## EVERY DOLLAR MAKES A DIFFERENCE

# the
# better
# world
## SHOPPING
## GUIDE

D0954608

new society
PUBLISHERS

**Cataloging in Publication Data:**
A catalog record for this publication is available from the National Library of Canada.

Cover concept by Ellis Jones. Design by Diane McIntosh.
Images: Getty Images/Photodisc Green.

Printed in Canada.

Paperback ISBN: 978-0-86571-724-4
eISBN: 978-1-55092-519-7

Inquiries regarding requests to reprint all or part of *The Better World Shopping Guide* should be addressed to New Society Publishers at the address below.

To order directly from the publishers, please call toll-free (North America) 1-800-567-6772, or order online at www.newsociety.com

Any other inquiries can be directed by mail to:
New Society Publishers
P.O. Box 189, Gabriola Island, BC V0R 1X0, Canada
1-800-567-6772

New Society Publishers' mission is to publish books that contribute in fundamental ways to building an ecologically sustainable and just society, and to do so with the least possible impact on the environment, in a manner that models this vision. We are committed to doing this not just through education, but through action. Our printed, bound books are printed on Forest Stewardship Council-certified acid-free paper that is **100% post-consumer recycled** (100% old growth forest-free), processed chlorine free, and printed with vegetable-based, low-VOC inks, with covers produced using FSC-certified stock. New Society also works to reduce its carbon footprint, and purchases carbon offsets based on an annual audit to ensure a carbon neutral footprint. For further information, or to browse our full list of books and purchase securely, visit our website at: www.newsociety.com

MIX
Paper from
responsible sources
FSC® C016245

# Contents

# APPRECIATION

I am very grateful to Paul Todisco, Collin Ahrens, Mark Fairbrother, Tom McGlynn, Jason Logan, Brett Jacobs, J.P. Meyer, Kristin Wallace, Jacob O'Brien and Warren Zeger for their hard work testing the guide and researching brands in the real world, and to my wife, Ara Francis, for her unwavering advocacy and dedication to getting this project the recognition and support it deserves. Also, a very special thank you to the good people at Christie Communications who have been incredible in making important connections for me around this work. Finally, my thanks to the good people at The Laughing Goat in Boulder, CO who provide a wonderful space for people to write, think, and order as many iced tea refills as one can safely consume.

I am also very grateful to you, the reader, for picking up this book. I'd like to say (because you may never hear it from anyone else) on behalf of all of the people on this planet whom you will never meet and all the natural places you will never see...

Thank you.

# 4TH EDITION NOTES

I must admit that I am still completely amazed at the idea that this little book has sold over 100,000 copies! I am deeply inspired when I think of the tens of thousands of people who have decided that our time has come to apply the lessons of democracy to our economy.

After surviving near financial meltdown, devastating oil spills, and enormous bank bailouts, we're finally beginning to understand the deep connection between our economic and our political lives. To bring about real change, we'll need some powerful tools. In this edition you'll find:

✓ More than 2000 companies evaluated
✓ Over 50 sources of reliable data cited
✓ A new product category! (Outdoor Gear)
✓ More Top 10 Lists (Successes, Failures)
✓ New Green Heroes & Corporate Villains
✓ A Frequently Asked Questions (FAQ) List
✓ An updated iPhone app! (not included)

Let's reclaim our democracy.

# THE WEBSITE

This guide is far too small to contain the wide range of data that goes into generating the rankings for each company. If you are interested in more specifics on how individual companies are rated, and exactly what is taken into account, you can visit the website. It also contains updated rankings, direct links to resources, and new product categories that have been added since the writing of this guide.

One other note that may be of interest to some of you is the release of an iPhone App called "Better World Shopper" based on the same data. While it does not provide all of the useful information you'll find in this book, it does give you instant access to all of the rankings. Having this information at your fingertips can turn out to be really useful, particularly when you forget to bring the book with you!

Learn more about the research behind this work and take a peek at the iPhone app online at:

www.betterworldshopper.org

# THE PROBLEM

Money is power. Perhaps more than any generation that has come before us, we understand the deeply-rooted reality of this short phrase and its universal meaning for every human being living on this planet.

It follows that wherever large amounts of money collect, so also new centers of power form. The latest historical manifestation of this is the modern corporation. As trillions of dollars accumulate in the corporate sphere, we witness the growing power of corporations to shape the world as they see fit.

This power is not limited to controlling the face of our own government through consistent, record-breaking, campaign contributions, but also the fate of millions of people and the planet itself through jobs, resource exploitation, pollution, working conditions, energy consumption, forest destruction, and so on.

Make no mistake, these new power centers are not democracies. We don't vote for the CEO's or their policies (unless we are rich enough to be significant shareholders, who are informed enough to know what's going on, and compassionate enough to care about more than just personal profit), yet our destinies are increasingly in their hands.

# THE SOLUTION

As these power centers shift, we must shift our own voices if we wish to be heard. As citizens, on average, we might vote once every four years, if at all. As consumers, we vote every single day with the purest form of power...money. The average American family spends around $22,000 every year on goods and services. Think of it as casting 22,000 votes every year for the kind of world you want to live in.

Unfortunately, as difficult as it is to find good, solid information on candidates during an election year, it's often even harder to find good, solid information on corporations. Our current laws are so lax, that half of the time we can't even figure out which brands belong to which companies (they don't have to tell us), much less have any idea of what their business practices look like.

For the past decade, I've dedicated myself to researching this very problem by compiling a database of every reliable source of information available on corporate behavior, and synthesizing the information into a single report card grade for every company. The result is this book. Use it to reclaim your true vote. Use it to build a better world.

# THE ISSUES

➤ **HUMAN RIGHTS:** sweatshops, third-world community exploitation, international health issues, economic divestment, child labor, worker health & safety records, union busting, fair wages, fatalities, democratic principles.

➤ **THE ENVIRONMENT:** global warming, toxic waste dumping, rainforest destruction, pollution, recycling, renewable energy, eco-innovations, sustainable farming, resource conservation, ecosystem impacts.

➤ **ANIMAL PROTECTION:** humane treatment, animal testing, utilization of alternatives, factory farming, animal habitat preservation, sustainable harvesting.

➤ **COMMUNITY INVOLVEMENT:** volunteer efforts, local business support, sustainable growth, family farms, donations, nonprofit alliances, campaign contributions, paid lobbyists, political corruption, greenwashing.

➤ **SOCIAL JUSTICE:** class action lawsuits, unethical business practices, government fines, cover-ups, illegal activities, transparency, harassment, discrimination based on race, gender, age, sexuality, ability, religion, ethnicity.

# THE SOURCES

Here is a short list of some of the resources used to assess the overall social responsibility of the companies included in this guide:

[BBB]   Better Business Bureau: Torch Awards
[BE]    Business Ethics: 100 Best Corporate Citizens
[CCC]   Clean Computer Campaign
[CC]    Climate Counts
[CEP]   Council on Economic Priorities
[CER]   Covalence Ethical Rankings
[CK]    Corporate Knights: 100 Most Sustainable Corporations
[CRP]   Center for Responsive Politics
[CW]    Corpwatch: Greenwash Awards
[EC]    Ethical Consumer: Rankings & Boycotts
[EPA]   US Environmental Protection Agency
[FT]    Transfair USA: Fair Trade Certification
[GAM]   Green America: Green Business Certification
[GP]    Greenpeace: Guide to Green Electronics
[HRC]   Human Rights Campaign: Equality Index
[MM]    Multinational Monitor: 10 Worst Corporations Annual List
[RS]    Responsible Shopper: Overall Social & Environmental Responsibility Rankings

For a more comprehensive list visit: www.betterworldshopper.org

# THE RANKINGS

**STEP 1:** Over 20 years worth of data is collected from a wide range of public, private, and nonprofit sources tracking information on one or more of the five issue areas that make up the overall responsibility picture for companies that create the products and services we use every day.

**STEP 2:** The data is organized into a massive database of more than 1000 companies that matches each individual company with its brands, assigns appropriate weights to each piece of data based on its quality, reliability, and scope, and calculates an overall social and environmental responsibility score for each company from −50 to +50.

**STEP 3:** Companies and brands are transferred to smaller, more specific data charts based on common product categories where each is assigned a letter grade based on its overall responsibility relative to its competitors in the same product category. This relative grading system allows consumers to maximize the impact of their dollars regardless of what they're purchasing.

# THE RANKINGS

**STEP 4:** Researchers are sent to supermarkets, natural foods stores, and retail outlets across the country to identify those products which are most commonly available to the average consumer to make sure that what you see on the shelves matches what you see in the book. Those particular companies/brands are then transferred into the easy-to-use report cards that make up the bulk of the shopping guide.

**STEP 5:** As regular data sources release their latest findings, they are added to the database. Also, as new third-party sources of data are identified, they are evaluated for potential inclusion in the ranking system. Mergers and buyouts are tracked so that their effects on the rankings can be noted. Updated rankings are regularly made available online through the website until a new edition of the shopping guide can be published.

As readers, your comments and suggestions are invaluable. Please contact me if you have ideas on how to improve the ranking system.

contact@betterworldshopper.org

# FREQUENTLY ASKED QUESTIONS

**"Isn't it more important to buy less stuff rather than worry about the kind of stuff we're buying?":** Both are equally important. As we've learned from the voluntary simplicity movement, we must reduce our *quantity* of consumption if we are to have any reasonable future. At the same time, we must increase the *quality* of our consumption so that every dollar spent helps build a better tomorrow rather than bring about its destruction. While I wholeheartedly support the former, this book deals mainly with the latter.

**"What if I don't have access to or can't afford many of the products that receive 'A' ratings?":** Don't give up! It's important to choose the best option available to you depending on your location and resources, both of which will likely change many times in your life. Sometimes the choice is between a 'C' brand and an 'F' brand, and that is just as important a choice to make. I, myself, strive to maintain an overall shopping GPA of 'B+' - and even then, I'm not always successful. Remember, as with voting, there is always a choice to be made, imperfect as it may be.

# FREQUENTLY ASKED QUESTIONS

**"Isn't this 'buying green' just something to make us feel better rather than something that will actually lead to real change?":** No. Trillions of dollars circulate in the global economy, driven primarily by consumers. These are our dollars that are shaping the fate of this world, and we must begin taking responsibility for their collective impact. Dollars (like votes) add up very quickly and can lead to powerful changes in both the short and long term.

**"Shouldn't we be voting, demonstrating, and organizing within our political system?":** Yes. We need to bring transparency, accountability and responsibility to both our political AND economic systems. If we address only one, our efforts will ultimately fail. So, do not use this guide as an excuse to shift focus away from our political problems - the two go hand in hand.

**"How do I find out more details about a particular company or the ranking system as a whole?":** Email me, or better yet, invite me out to come talk about it!

# BEST COMPANY PROFILE (BANKS)

# NEW RESOURCE BANK

☆ Green America Certified Green Business
☆ San Francisco Certified Green Business
☆ Social Venture Network member
☆ A Certified "B Corporation"
☆ 100% Wind Power, EPA Certified
☆ LEED Gold Certified headquarters
☆ American Sustainable Business Council member
☆ Car sharing program offered to all employees for meetings
☆ Offers a debit card that donates to environmental orgs with each purchase

OVERALL GRADE: A+

www.newresourcebank.com

# WORST COMPANY PROFILE (BANKS)

# CITIBANK

- ☠ Recipient, Corporate Shame Award[3]
- ☠ Worst overall ranking in industry[43]
- ☠ Worst Corporations List for 2 years[38]
- ☠ 'D' for social & environmental impacts[52]
- ☠ Overall ethics rating of VERY POOR[22]
- ☠ $50 billion paid by us to bailout[41]
- ☠ $85 million paid to political lobbyists[8]
- ☠ $30 million in campaign contributions[8]
- ☠ $2.7 billion to settle WorldCom fraud[41]
- ☠ SEC — Citi helped Enron commit fraud[36]
- ☠ Sued for selling worthless Enron stock[43]
- ☠ Paid largest settlement in FTC history[36]
- ☠ GAO — negligent of money laundering[49]
- ☠ $70 million paid for unfair lending[43]

OVERALL GRADE:  F

*For more details you can look up the source reference
number in the DATA SOURCES section in the back.*

# THE 20 BEST LIST

1. SEVENTH GENERATION
2. METHOD
3. ORGANIC VALLEY
4. PATAGONIA
5. EQUAL EXCHANGE
6. ALTER ECO
7. DR. BRONNER'S
8. TRADITIONAL MEDICINALS
9. EO BODYCARE
10. CLIF BAR
11. NEW BELGIUM BREWING
12. G DIAPERS
13. DANSKO
14. KING ARTHUR FLOUR
15. EDEN FOODS
16. EARTH FRIENDLY
17. MAGGIE'S ORGANICS
18. NATURE'S PATH
19. WORKING ASSETS
20. DIVINE CHOCOLATE

Rankings are based on overall social and environmental records

# THE 20 WORST LIST

1. EXXON-MOBIL
2. KRAFT (& ALTRIA)
3. WALMART
5. GENERAL ELECTRIC
6. GENERAL MOTORS
4. CHEVRON-TEXACO
7. NESTLE
8. PFIZER
9. VERIZON
10. CITIBANK
11. AIG
12. BLUE CROSS / BLUE SHIELD
13. ARCHER DANIELS MIDLAND
14. MICROSOFT
15. DOW CHEMICAL
16. PROCTER & GAMBLE
17. HOFFMANN-LA ROCHE
18. BANK OF AMERICA
19. GEORGIA PACIFIC (KOCH)
20. TYSON FOODS

Rankings are based on overall social and environmental records

# THE 10 SMALL BUT BEAUTIFUL LIST

1. GUAYAKI
2. BETTER WORLD TELECOM
3. NEW RESOURCE BANK
4. NUMI TEA
5. NEW LEAF PAPER
6. RECYCLINE (PRESERVE)
7. GROUNDS FOR CHANGE
8. CARE2.COM
9. BETTER WORLD CLUB
10. PANGEA ORGANICS

The above list includes 10 small companies you may not have heard of that are true social and environmental leaders in their industries.

# THE TOP 10 THINGS TO CHANGE

1. BANK
2. GASOLINE
3. SUPERMARKET
4. RETAIL STORES
5. CAR
6. SEAFOOD
7. CHOCOLATE
8. COFFEE / TEA
9. CREDIT CARDS
10. CLEANING PRODUCTS

If you want to begin with the changes that will make the most difference for people and the planet, start with these ten things.

# THE 10 BIGGEST SUCCESS STORIES

| *GRADE CHANGE* | *'06* ▸ *'12* |
|---|---|
| 1. EO PRODUCTS | B+ ▸ A+ |
| 2. GREEN FOREST | B ▸ A+ |
| 3. SAN-J | C ▸ A |
| 4. SOUTHWEST AIR | D+ ▸ B+ |
| 5. OFFICE DEPOT | D- ▸ B |
| 6. DANSKO | ** ▸ A+ |
| 7. METHOD | ** ▸ A+ |
| 8. PANGEA ORGANICS | ** ▸ A+ |
| 9. CHIPOTLE | ** ▸ A |
| 10. KIMPTON HOTELS | ** ▸ A |

The above list includes the 5 companies that, as of July 2012, have shown the most improvement since the 1st edition of the book was released, as well as 5 companies that weren't listed in the original edition (noted by **). Every one of these companies is a demonstration of what a deep commitment to a better world can achieve in a mere 6 years.

# THE 10 BIGGEST DISAPPOINTMENTS

*GRADE CHANGE*     *'06* ▶ *'12*

| | | |
|---|---|---|
| 1. SILK | A⁺ ▶ C |
| 2. HORIZON ORGANIC | A ▶ C |
| 3. BURT'S BEES | A⁻ ▶ C⁺ |
| 4. BP | A⁻ ▶ D⁻ |
| 5. FEDEX | B ▶ D |
| 6. CADBURY | B⁻ ▶ F |
| 7. GERBER | C⁺ ▶ F |
| 8. UNILEVER | C ▶ F |
| 9. PROCTER & GAMBLE | C ▶ F |
| 10. BANK OF AMERICA | C⁻ ▶ F |

The above list includes the 10 companies that, as of July 2012, have fallen from the top of their respective industries to the middle, or worse, from the middle to the very bottom. It is essential that we, as consumers, send a clear message that we will no longer reward companies for this kind of irresponsible behavior.

# THE TOP 10 BAILOUT LIST

| | | |
|---|---|---:|
| 1. | AIG | 70 |
| 2. | CITIBANK | 50 |
| 3. | BANK OF AMERICA | 45 |
| 4. | GENERAL MOTORS | 31 |
| 5. | JP MORGAN | 25 |
| 6. | WELLS FARGO | 25 |
| 7. | CHRYSLER | 12 |
| 8. | MORGAN STANLEY | 10 |
| 9. | GOLDMAN SACHS | 10 |
| 10. | PNC FINANCIAL | 8 |

We are quickly learning that unless we, as consumers, can keep companies responsible in the marketplace, we may end up paying for their irresponsible behavior with our own taxpayer dollars.

The above list includes the 10 companies that, as of May 2009, received the most bailout money from the US taxpayers. The figures on the right represent how much we have spent, *in billions*, bailing these companies out.[41]

# THE TOP 10 LOBBYIST LIST

1. GENERAL ELECTRIC 274
2. KRAFT (& ALTRIA) 208
3. AT&T 205
4. EXXON MOBIL 176
5. BLUE CROSS/SHIELD 191
6. VERIZON 168
7. GENERAL MOTORS 132
8. PFIZER 126
9. FORD 101
10. MICROSOFT 98

It's important to understand that we are not the only ones learning to turn our dollars into votes. These are some of the loudest economic voices in Washington.

The above list includes 10 companies currently spending some of the largest amounts of money on Washington lobbyists to influence the democratic process in ways that serve their own interests. The figures on the right represent how much they have spent, *in millions*, over the last fifteen years.[8]

# WHAT DO THE GRADES MEAN?

| | |
|---|---|
| **A** | Often these companies were created specifically to provide socially and environmentally responsible options for consumers. A handful are merely responsibility leaders in their industry. |
| **B** | These tend to represent mainstream companies that are making significant progress in turning toward more people/planet friendly behaviors. |
| **C** | Companies that fall in the middle either have mixed responsibility records or insufficient data exists to rank them relative to the other companies. |
| **D** | If a company ends up here, it is involved in practices that have significantly negative consequences for humans and the environment. |
| **F** | This category is reserved for companies that are actively participating in the rapid destruction of the planet and the exploitation of human beings. Avoid these products at all costs. |

# WHAT IS ALL THIS EXTRA STUFF?

**WHAT YOU NEED TO KNOW**
This section will give you a thumbnail sketch of the current industry and its impact.

**BUYING TIPS**
Here you'll see tips that should help you maximize the positive impact of your dollar.

**GREEN HERO**

## Company X

Examples of just a few of the things that put this particular company head and shoulders above the rest.

**CORPORATE VILLAIN**

## Company Y

Examples of some of the things that land this company squarely at the bottom of the rankings.

**RESOURCES**
Here you'll find web links to sites that provide you with more information on the best companies or practices.

# WHAT IF I CAN'T FIND A COMPANY?

While this guide is meant to be comprehensive, it is far from complete. You will likely encounter companies and brands on the shelves that don't show up in these pages. Here are a few simple guidelines that should help you:

If an unknown company's products are certified fair trade, you may assume that it falls into the A- range.

If an unknown company's products are certified organic, you may assume that it falls into the B+ range.

If you don't know anything at all about a particular company or brand, assume that it falls into the C range.

Unknown companies producing clothing, electronics, or shoes should be assumed to have a D or F.

If you wish to see a more detailed version of these rankings or ask about a particular company that you can't find in the guide, you're welcome to visit:

www.betterworldshopper.org

# HOW TO USE THIS SHOPPING GUIDE

This book is meant to be used as a practical guide while shopping at the supermarket, in the mall, or online. Familiarize yourself with the alphabetical listing of categories and "dog-ear" any pages you find particularly useful.

Utilize the rankings on the left as a quick guide to any product you're thinking about buying. Note that all rankings are relative to their product category so that a company may shift up or down depending on its competition.

Useful information and helpful tips appear on the right along with a quick sketch of some of the differences between the best and worst companies. At the bottom of the page are links to online resources to learn more about some of the companies listed.

The book has been purposefully made small so that you can keep it with you in your purse, backpack, briefcase, or pocket. Find a convenient place for it now, while you're reading this sentence. Whatever you do, don't put it on a shelf!

# AIRLINES

| | | |
|---|---|---|
| **A** | **A+** | |
| | **A** | |
| | **A−** | |
| **B** | **B+** | JetBlue, Southwest |
| | **B** | Alaska Air, Horizon |
| | **B−** | Frontier, Virgin |
| **C** | **C+** | Spirit, Easy Jet |
| | **C** | KLM, Air France, Cathay Pacific, Qantas, Singapore, Japan Airlines, Lufthansa, British Airways |
| | **C−** | Korean Air, SAS, AirTran, Aer Lingus, Air Canada, Air New Zealand, Express Jet, Sky West |
| **D** | **D+** | |
| | **D** | Delta |
| | **D−** | American Airlines, American Eagle |
| **F** | **F** | United, US Airways |

# AIRLINES

**WHAT YOU NEED TO KNOW**
Air travel has become so ubiquitous.in our modern society that we often forget its significant environmental impact.

**BUYING TIPS**
✓ Green travel organizations now offer carbon offsets to offset your flight's greenhouse gas emissions

**GREEN HERO**

## JetBlue

☆ 90 out of 100 on HRC Equality Index
☆ Industry leader in treatment of passengers
☆ Offers carbon offsets & green food options

**CORPORATE VILLAIN**

## United

☠ RS "F" for recycling efforts in the industry[43]
☠ Paid $55 million to Washington lobbyists[8]
☠ Named global climate change laggard[10]

**RESOURCES**
🖥 sustainabletravelinternational.org
🖥 www.terrapass.com

# APPLIANCES & HARDWARE

| | | |
|---|---|---|
| **A** | **A+** | Preserve, Recycline, TerraCycle |
| | **A** | Old Fashioned Milk Paint |
| | **A–** | |
| **B** | **B+** | |
| | **B** | Ace Hardware |
| | **B–** | WD-40, Owens Corning, Electrolux, Frigidaire, Norelco, Sony |
| **C** | **C+** | Stanley, Dyson, Miele, 3M, Tefal, Rubbermaid, Tupperware |
| | **C** | DeWalt, JCB, Dremel, BSH, Wahl, Krups, Sunbeam, Bissell, DeLonghi, Remington, Cuisinart, Magic Chef, Hoover, Dirt Devil, Conair, Siemens |
| | **C–** | Maytag, Whirlpool, Haier, Sylvania, Panasonic, Admiral, Kitchenaid, Sanyo, Black & Decker, Bosch |
| **D** | **D+** | Sherwin Williams, Acme, Dutch Boy, Braun, Samsung, Philips, Hitachi |
| | **D** | Home Depot |
| | **D–** | Lowe's, Emerson, LG, Daewoo |
| **F** | **F** | Sears, Walmart, Braun, Craftsman, Kenmore, GE, Costco |

# APPLIANCES & HARDWARE

**WHAT YOU NEED TO KNOW**
Whether it's major home improvement efforts or just small kitchen appliances, the hardware you buy for your house has a significant impact on the people abroad that help manufacture it.

**BUYING TIPS**
✓ Look for products with Energy Star labels

**CORPORATE VILLAIN**

## Walmart

☠ MM's "Worst Corporation" list for 3 years[38]
☠ Major toxic waste dumping fines[18]
☠ CEP "F" for overall social responsibility[9]
☠ Documented exploitation of child labor[43]

**CORPORATE VILLAIN**

## GE (General Electric)

☠ MM's "Worst Corporation" list for 5 years[38]
☠ #34 in "Top 100 Corporate Criminals"[38]
☠ Target of "War Profiteer" campaign[43]
☠ Paid $274 million to Washington lobbyists[8]

**RESOURCES**
⌨ www.energystar.gov

# BABY CARE

| | | |
|---|---|---|
| **A** | **A+** | Seventh Generation, gDiapers |
| | **A** | Earth Mama, Peapods, Healthy Times, Plum Organics, Happy Baby |
| | **A–** | Organic Baby, Tender Care, Tushies, Earth's Best, Ella's Kitchen, Jason |
| **B** | **B+** | Nature's Gate, Weleda |
| | **B** | Baby Magic |
| | **B–** | GoodNites, Huggies, Mr. Bubble |
| **C** | **C+** | Aveeno, Johnson & Johnson, Burt's Bees, Horizon Organic |
| | **C** | Graco, Pure n' Gentle, Munchkin |
| | **C–** | Avent, Enfamil, Oshkosh, Britax, Chicco, Evenflo, Playmates, Beech-Nut, Nature's Goodness, Carter's |
| **D** | **D+** | Bourdreaux's, Coppertone, Playtex, Del Monte, Church & Dwight, Arm & Hammer, Babies R Us |
| | **D** | |
| | **D–** | Pedialyte, Pediasure, Similac, Chiquita, Disney, Baby Einstein |
| **F** | **F** | Gerber, Nestle, Luvs, Q-Tips, Under Jams, Vaseline, Nabisco, Pampers |

# BABY CARE

**WHAT YOU NEED TO KNOW**

Infants and toddlers are more vulnerable to the effects of harmful chemicals and pesticides, so if you're going to buy anything organic, it should be something from this category.

**GREEN HERO**

## Seventh Generation

☆ Ranked #1 best company on the planet
☆ Empowers consumers w/packaging
☆ Winner, Sustainability Report Award
☆ Socially Responsible Business Award

**CORPORATE VILLAIN**

## Gerber (Nestle)

☠ Baby formula human rights boycott[36]
☠ "Most Irresponsible" corporation award[3]
☠ Involved in child slavery lawsuit[43]
☠ Aggressive takeovers of family farms[43]

**RESOURCES**

🖳 www.seventhgeneration.com
🖳 www.gdiapers.com
🖳 www.healthytimes.com
🖳 www.earthmamaangelbaby.com
🖳 www.peapods.com
🖳 www.happybabyfood.com

# BAKED GOODS & BAKING SUPPLIES

| | | |
|---|---|---|
| **A** | **A+** | King Arthur, Eden, Nature's Path |
| | **A** | Bob's Red Mill |
| | **A−** | Rapunzel, Spectrum, Arrowhead Mills, Ener-G, Hain |
| **B** | **B+** | Vermont Bread Co, Betty Crocker, Pillsbury, Gold Medal, Bisquick, Progresso |
| | **B** | Quaker, Mother's, Sun-Maid |
| | **B−** | Eagle Brand |
| **C** | **C+** | Ghirardelli, Krusteaz, Dr. Oetker |
| | **C** | Entenmann's, Karo, Cake Mate |
| | **C−** | Keebler, Kellogg's, Little Debbie, Hodgson Mills |
| **D** | **D+** | Contadina, Arm & Hammer, Hostess, Diamond |
| | **D** | Hershey's |
| | **D−** | Banquet |
| **F** | **F** | Duncan Hines, Jell-O, Nabisco, Borden, Kraft, Planters, Nestle, Carnation, Albers, Libby's |

# BAKED GOODS & BAKING SUPPLIES

**BUYING TIPS**
✓ Buy organic baking products when available

**GREEN HERO**
## King Arthur Flour

☆ 100% employee-owned company
☆ Awarded "Most Democratic Workplace"
☆ Business Ethics award winner
☆ B Lab Certified Responsible Company
☆ BBB's Torch Award for ethics

**CORPORATE VILLAIN**
## Jell-O (Kraft)

♟ MM's "Worst Corporation" list for 5 years[38]
♟ Currently target of 2 major boycotts[16,40]
♟ Greenwash Award for public deception[18]
♟ Named global climate change laggard[10]
♟ Paid $208 million to Washington lobbyists[8]

**RESOURCES**
🖳 www.edenfoods.com
🖳 www.kingarthurflour.com
🖳 www.naturespath.com
🖳 www.rapunzel.de/uk/
🖳 www.bobsredmill.com

# BANKS & CREDIT CARDS

| | | |
|---|---|---|
| **A** | **A+** | One Pacific Coast Bank, University Bank, New Resource Bank, VanCity |
| | **A** | Chittenden, Wainwright, Albina Green Choice, City First, Franklin |
| | **A–** | Working Assets, Green America, Brighter Planet |
| **B** | **B+** | |
| | **B** | LOCAL CREDIT UNIONS |
| | **B–** | |
| **C** | **C+** | American Express, TD Bank, ING |
| | **C** | Mastercard, HSBC, Northern Trust |
| | **C–** | Discover, Sovereign, Capital One |
| **D** | **D+** | VISA, US Bank, Credit Suisse, Fifth Third, UBS, Comerica, KeyBank |
| | **D** | Wells Fargo, SunTrust, Citizens |
| | **D–** | Chase, JP Morgan, Barclay's, Goldman Sachs |
| **F** | **F** | Bank Of America, Citibank |

# BANKS & CREDIT CARDS

**WHAT YOU NEED TO KNOW**

Where you put your money when you're not spending it is just as important as responsibly choosing what you spend it on. For your whole life (even while you sleep), that money will either be building a better world or tearing it down. Small, local banks and credit unions are typically your best bet. While shopping, make each purchase doubly effective by using a credit card that donates a percentage of your purchases (over $5500/yr for the average American) to saving the planet.

**BUYING TIPS**

✓ Try using both a local bank AND an 'A' bank
✓ Find out which credit unions are in your area
✓ Switch to a socially responsible credit card

**RESOURCES**

🖥 www.universitybank.com
🖥 www.newresourcebank.com
🖥 www.creditunion.coop/cu_locator
🖥 www.workingassets.com/creditcard
🖥 www.breakupwithyourmegabank.org

# BEER

| | | |
|---|---|---|
| **A** | **A+** | New Belgium |
| | **A** | Sierra Nevada, Wolaver's, Bison |
| | **A−** | ORGANIC / LOCAL BREWERIES |
| **B** | **B+** | Samuel Smith's, St. Peter's, Allagash |
| | **B** | Rogue, Full Sail, Pyramid, Anchor Steam, Harpoon, Alaskan, Magic Hat |
| | **B−** | |
| **C** | **C+** | Pabst, Stroh's, Schlitz, Old Milwaukee, Widmer, Redhook, Kona |
| | **C** | Keystone, Newcastle, Heineken, Amstel, Dos Equis, Asahi, Carlsberg |
| | **C−** | Coors, Corona, Miller, Modelo, Pacifico, Molson, Blue Moon |
| **D** | **D+** | Milwaukee's Best, Samuel Adams, Leinenkugel, Grolsch, Foster's |
| | **D** | Guinness, Harp, Red Stripe |
| | **D−** | Budweiser, Michelob, Rolling Rock, Becks, Stella Artois, Bass, Busch, Lowenbrau, Kirin, Natural Light |
| **F** | **F** | |

# BEER

**BUYING TIPS**
✓ Look for organic varieties of beer
✓ Buy from local microbreweries when possible
✓ Avoid buying beer in plastic bottles

**GREEN HERO**

## New Belgium

☆ 1st 100% wind-powered brewery
☆ Conserves 50% more water vs. average
☆ An employee-owned business
☆ 4x Awarded "Most Democratic Workplace"
☆ $1.6 million donated to local community

**CORPORATE VILLAIN**

## Budweiser (Anheuser-Busch InBev)

☠ #41 of PERI 100 Most Toxic Air Polluters[42]
☠ Paid $32 million to Washington lobbyists[8]
☠ EC overall responsibility rating of POOR[22]

**RESOURCES**
💻 www.newbelgium.com
💻 www.sierranevada.com
💻 www.ottercreekbrewing.com
💻 www.bisonbrew.com
💻 www.craftbeer.com

# BODY CARE

| | | |
|---|---|---|
| **A** | **A+** | Preserve, Dr. Bronner's, Method, EO, Tweezerman, Pangea Organics |
| | **A** | Aubrey, EcoLips, Auromere, Allen's, Aura Cacia, Kiss My Face |
| | **A–** | Lush, Dr Hauschka, Body Shop, Zia, Aveda, Tom's of Maine |
| **B** | **B+** | Pure & Basic, Ecco Bella, Giovanni, Jäsön, Alba, Nature's Gate, Shikai |
| | **B** | Avalon, Desert Essence, Crystal, Colgate, Speed Stick, Mennen |
| | **B–** | Ban, CO Bigelow, Jergens, Biore |
| **C** | **C+** | Bic, Burt's Bees, Lubriderm, Aveeno, Neutrogena, Clean & Clear, Purell |
| | **C** | Barbasol, Banana Boat |
| | **C–** | Schick, Nivea, Blistex, Edge |
| **D** | **D+** | Coppertone, Arrid, Arm & Hammer |
| | **D** | Keri, Curel |
| | **D–** | Right Guard, Dry Idea, Soft & Dri |
| **F** | **F** | Dove, Suave, Vaseline, Degree, Axe, Mitchum, Chapstick, Noxema, Sure, Old Spice, Secret, Gillette, Oil of Olay, St. Ives |

# BODY CARE

**BUYING TIPS**
- ✓ Avoid products tested on animals
- ✓ Seek out items made with organic ingredients
- ✓ Look for recyclable containers — #1, #2 plastic
- ✓ Buy larger quantities to reduce packaging

**GREEN HERO**

## Pangea Organics

- ☆ GAM certified Green Business
- ☆ Never tests ingredients on animals
- ☆ 2x Award Winner for Business Ethics

**CORPORATE VILLAIN**

## Chapstick (Pfizer)

- ☠ #41 of PERI 100 Most Toxic Air Polluters[42]
- ☠ #17 in "Top 100 Corporate Criminals"[38]
- ☠ MM's "Worst Corporation" list for 4 years[38]
- ☠ Paid $126 million to Washington lobbyists[8]

**RESOURCES**
- 💻 www.pangeaorganics.com
- 💻 www.eoproducts.com
- 💻 www.recycline.com
- 💻 www.drbronner.com
- 💻 www.tweezerman.com

# BREAD

| | | |
|---|---|---|
| **A** | **A+** | LOCAL BAKERY, Nature's Path |
| | **A** | Alvarado St Bakery, Food For Life |
| | **A−** | Ener-G, Rudi's Organic, Vermont Bread Co., Great Harvest Bread Co. |
| **B** | **B+** | Gold Medal, Pillsbury, Barowsky's, Colombo, Betty Crocker |
| | **B** | Sun-Maid |
| | **B−** | Pepperidge Farm |
| **C** | **C+** | La Brea |
| | **C** | Boboli, Oroweat, Tia Rosa, Thomas', Arnold, Freihofer's, Country Hearth, Milton's, FiberOne, Roman Meal |
| | **C−** | Mission, Weight Watchers |
| **D** | **D+** | Lender's, Van De Kamp's, Sara Lee, Rainbo, Earth Grains, Ball Park, Wonder, Home Pride, Nature's Pride |
| | **D** | |
| | **D−** | Alexia |
| **F** | **F** | Kraft, Stove-Top |

# BREAD

**WHAT YOU NEED TO KNOW**
Despite all of our technological advancement, it's still a challenge to find a good, socially responsible loaf of bread in the supermarket.

**BUYING TIPS**
✓ Support a local bakery in your community

**GREEN HERO**

## Alvarado Street Bakery

☆ Worker-owned cooperative
☆ PC socially responsible business award
☆ GAM certified Green Business

**CORPORATE VILLAIN**

## Wonder (Hostess)

☠ $18 million settlement for securities fraud[36]
☠ Refused disclosure to consumers[36]
☠ CEP "F" for overall social responsibility[9]

**RESOURCES**
⌨ www.naturespath.com
⌨ www.alvaradostreetbakery.com
⌨ www.rudisbakery.com
⌨ www.foodforlife.com

# BREAKFAST FOOD

| | | |
|---|---|---|
| **A** | **A+** | Nature's Path, Envirokidz |
| | **A** | Amy's Kitchen |
| | **A−** | |
| **B** | **B+** | General Mills, Betty Crocker, Van's, Pillsbury, Batter Blaster, Shelton's |
| | **B** | Quaker |
| | **B−** | Smucker's, Hungry Jack |
| **C** | **C+** | Krusteaz |
| | **C** | Entenmann's, Farm Rich, Ian's |
| | **C−** | Morningstar Farms, Eggo, Kashi, Bob Evans, Weight Watchers, Kellogg's |
| **D** | **D+** | Jimmy Dean, Aunt Jemima, Armour Log Cabin, Mrs. Butterworth's, Ore-Ida, Hormel, Swanson, Bird's Eye |
| | **D** | |
| | **D−** | PAM, Banquet |
| **F** | **F** | Nestle, Kraft, Nabisco, Boca, Golden Griddle, Skippy, Kudos |

# BREAKFAST FOOD

**WHAT YOU NEED TO KNOW**
Every morning of your life, what you put on your plate for breakfast will determine what kind of world your children inherit in the future.

**BUYING TIPS**
✓ Buy at least one organic item for breakfast

**GREEN HERO**

## Amy's Kitchen

☆ Donates food to relief efforts
☆ Produces all-vegetarian, organic foods
☆ GAM certified Green Business

**CORPORATE VILLAIN**

## PAM (ConAgra)

☠ #50 in "Top 100 Corporate Criminals"[38]
☠ Ceres "Climate Change Laggard"[10]
☠ CEP "F" for overall social responsibility[9]
☠ Low score on HRC Equality Index[35]

**RESOURCES**
🖳 www.amyskitchen.com
🖳 www.envirokidz.com
🖳 www.naturespath.com

# BUTTER & MARGARINE

| A | A+ | Organic Valley, Organic Pastures, Straus Family Creamery |
| | A | |
| | A− | Spectrum |
| B | B+ | Clover Stornetta |
| | B | Cabot |
| | B− | Smart Balance, Earth Balance |
| C | C+ | Challenge, Benecol |
| | C | Land O' Lakes, Canoleo, Kerrygold, Cloverleaf, Saffola, Nucoa, Canola Harvest, Horizon Organic, Crystal |
| | C− | Tillamook |
| D | D+ | |
| | D | |
| | D− | Blue Bonnet, Fleischmann's, Parkay |
| F | F | Brummel & Brown, I Can't Believe It's Not Butter, Willow Run, Shedd's, Country Crock, Imperial, Promise |

# BUTTER & MARGARINE

**BUYING TIPS**

✓ Look for "No Hormones" and "No Antibiotics"
✓ Seek out items made with organic ingredients
✓ Avoid hydrogenated, saturated, and trans fats

**GREEN HERO**

## Organic Valley

☆ Small family farmer-owned co-operative
☆ Gives 10% of profits to local community
☆ Humane animal treatment a priority
☆ Ranked #3 best company on the planet

**CORPORATE VILLAIN**

## Parkay (ConAgra)

☠ #50 in "Top 100 Corporate Criminals"[38]
☠ CEP "F" for overall social responsibility[9]
☠ Ceres "Climate Change Laggard"[10]
☠ Low score on HRC Equality Index[35]

**RESOURCES**

⌨ www.organicvalley.coop
⌨ www.strausmilk.com
⌨ www.organicpastures.com
⌨ www.cornucopia.org

# CANDY, GUM & MINTS

| | | |
|---|---|---|
| **A** | **A+** | |
| | **A** | Glee Gum, Sencha Natural |
| | **A–** | Speakeasy, Hain, St. Claire's |
| **B** | **B+** | Newman's Own, Ginger People |
| | **B** | |
| | **B–** | Red Vines |
| **C** | **C+** | Panda, Haribo, La Vie |
| | **C** | Tootsie Roll, Charm's, Mike & Ike, Werthers, Tic Tacs, Mentos, Andes |
| | **C–** | |
| **D** | **D+** | Jelly Belly |
| | **D** | Hershey's, Heath, Mounds, Reese's, Kit Kat, Almond Joy, Twizzlers |
| | **D–** | Twix, Starburst, Skittles, M&Ms, Snickers, Milky Way, 3 Musketeers, LifeSavers, Mars, Extra, Orbit |
| **F** | **F** | Kraft, Cadbury, Trolli, Nerds, Nestle, Butterfinger, Wonka, SweeTarts, After Eight, Certs, Dentyne, Trident |

# CANDY, GUM & MINTS

**BUYING TIPS**

Most major candy manufacturers are also major chocolate purchasers, which currently means that they are using child slave labor to produce much of their candy. It's important to keep these companies accountable until they agree to basic human rights standards in the industry.

**GREEN HERO**

## Glee Gum

☆ GAM certified Green Business
☆ Uses wild-harvested rainforest plants
☆ Actively supports environmental groups

**CORPORATE VILLAIN**

## M&Ms (Mars)

☠ On MM's "10 Worst Corporations" list[38]
☠ Evidence of involvement in child slave labor[43]
☠ Target of international fair trade campaign[18]

**RESOURCES**

🖥 www.gleegum.com
🖥 www.stclaires.com

# CANNED BEANS, CHILI & STEWS

| | | |
|---|---|---|
| **A** | **A+** | Eden Foods |
| | **A** | Amy's Kitchen |
| | **A−** | Walnut Acres, Westbrae, Bearitos |
| **B** | **B+** | Progresso, Old El Paso, Hamburger Helper, Shelton's |
| | **B** | |
| | **B−** | Campbell's |
| **C** | **C+** | |
| | **C** | Bush's, B&M, Nalley, Ortega, GOYA |
| | **C−** | |
| **D** | **D+** | S&W, Heinz, Hormel, Dinty Moore, Stagg |
| | **D** | |
| | **D−** | Dennison's, Rosarita, Van Camp's, Marie Callender's |
| **F** | **F** | Libby's, Taco Bell, Knorr |

# CANNED BEANS, CHILI & STEWS

**WHAT YOU NEED TO KNOW**

Some of the most socially responsible companies now provide a wide variety of canned goods that should be available at most supermarkets.

**GREEN HERO**

## Eden Foods

☆ Ranked #15 best company on the planet
☆ CEP's highest social responsibility score
☆ GAM certified Green Business

**CORPORATE VILLAIN**

## Hormel

☠ Suppliers linked to inhumane practices[36]
☠ Low score on HRC Equality Index[35]
☠ Refuses disclosure to consumers[29]

**RESOURCES**

🖥 www.edenfoods.com
🖥 www.amyskitchen.com
🖥 www.westbrae.com
🖥 www.walnutacres.com

# CANNED FRUIT & VEGETABLES

| | | |
|---|---|---|
| **A** | **A+** | Eden Foods |
| | **A** | |
| | **A−** | Muir Glen, Westbrae, Native Forest |
| **B** | **B+** | Natural Value, Santa Cruz Organic |
| | **B** | Progresso, Green Giant, Sunsweet, Tree Top |
| | **B−** | |
| **C** | **C+** | Ocean Spray |
| | **C** | Oregon, Glory Foods |
| | **C−** | Mott's |
| **D** | **D+** | Del Monte, S&W, Contadina |
| | **D** | Dole, French's |
| | **D−** | Hunt's |
| **F** | **F** | Libby's |

# CANNED FRUIT & VEGETABLES

**WHAT YOU NEED TO KNOW**

While "organic" has become increasingly popular in fresh produce sections of supermarkets, there is a small, but growing, selection of canned fruits and vegetables available on the aisle shelves.

**GREEN HERO**

## Muir Glen

☆ First organic tomato processor in US
☆ Environmental leader in food industry
☆ GAM certified Green Business

**CORPORATE VILLAIN**

## Libby's (Kraft)

☠ Greenwash Award for public deception[18]
☠ Named global climate change laggard[10]
☠ Currently target of 2 major boycotts[16,40]
☠ Paid $208 million to Washington lobbyists[8]
☠ MM's "Worst Corporation" list for 5 years[38]

**RESOURCES**

🖥 www.muirglen.com
🖥 www.edenfoods.com
🖥 www.scojuice.com

# CARS

| A | A+ | |
| | A | |
| | A– | |
| B | B+ | |
| | B | Toyota, Lexus, Scion, Honda, Acura |
| | B– | Volkswagen, Audi, Bentley |
| C | C+ | Hyundai, Kia |
| | C | Subaru, Smart Car, Fiat, Peugeot, Renault, BMW, Mini, Volvo |
| | C– | Mazda, Mercedes, Ferrari, Porsche |
| D | D+ | Isuzu, Tata, Suzuki |
| | D | Nissan, Infiniti |
| | D– | Mitsubishi |
| F | F | Chrysler, General Motors, Jeep, Dodge, Ford, GMC, Lincoln, Mercury, Buick, Cadillac, Saturn, Chevrolet, Saab, Hummer, Jaguar, Land Rover |

# CARS

**BUYING TIPS:**
✓ Look for cars that get at least 30 MPG
✓ Think about a hybrid vehicle for your next car
✓ Consider buying carbon offsets for your car

**CORPORATE VILLAIN**

## Chrysler

☠ UCS worst environmental auto ranking[47]
☠ Paid $54 million to Washington lobbyists[8]
☠ #53 of PERI 100 Most Toxic Air Polluters[42]
☠ *$12 billion* paid by taxpayers to bailout[41]

**CORPORATE VILLAIN**

## General Motors

☠ Leader in fighting clean air legislation[43]
☠ Paid $132 million to Washington lobbyists[8]
☠ MM's "Worst Corporation" list for 4 years[38]
☠ *$31 billion* paid by taxpayers to bailout[41]

**RESOURCES**
🖳 www.fueleconomy.gov
🖳 www.betterworldclub.com
🖳 www.terrapass.com

# CELL PHONES & SERVICE

| | | |
|---|---|---|
| **A** | **A+** | Better World Telecom, Credo, Working Assets |
| | **A** | Earth Tones |
| | **A–** | |
| **B** | **B+** | Apple |
| | **B** | Nokia |
| | **B–** | Sony |
| **C** | **C+** | Ericsson |
| | **C** | Motorola, STI Mobile, TracFone, US Cellular, MetroPCS, Siemens, Jabra, Kyocera, Boost Mobile, Cricket |
| | **C–** | Sanyo, Audiovox |
| **D** | **D+** | BlackBerry, T-Mobile, Sprint, Nextel, Virgin, Samsung |
| | **D** | LG |
| | **D–** | AT&T, Acer |
| **F** | **F** | Verizon, Windows Mobile |

# CELL PHONES & SERVICE

**WHAT YOU NEED TO KNOW**
Cell phones are part of a billion dollar industry.
Make sure that this significant revenue stream
is going toward building a better world rather
than tearing it apart.

**BUYING TIPS**
✓ Remember to recycle your old cell phone(s)
✓ Look for solar chargers to reduce energy use

**GREEN HERO**
## Credo (Working Assets)

☆ Given $60 million to a range of nonprofits
☆ Purchases carbon offsets for energy use
☆ Educates for engaged citizenship

**CORPORATE VILLAIN**
## Verizon

☠ Given $168 million to Washington lobbyists[8]
☠ CEP "F" for overall social responsibility[9]
☠ Discriminated against pregnant employees[36]

**RESOURCES**
🖳 betterworldtelecom.com
🖳 www.workingassets.com
🖳 www.earthtones.com

# CEREAL

| | | |
|---|---|---|
| **A** | A+ | Nature's Path, Envirokidz |
| | A | Bob's Red Mill, Alvarado Street, Food For Life |
| | A− | Barbara's, Peace Cereal, Arrowhead Mills, Health Valley, Earth's Best |
| **B** | B+ | Lundberg, Newman's Own Organic, Cascadian Farm, General Mills, Pillsbury, Wheaties, Nature Valley, Cheerios, Chex, Total, Kix |
| | B | Quaker, Mother's |
| | B− | |
| **C** | C+ | |
| | C | Malt-O-Meal, Cream of Wheat |
| | C− | Kelloggs, Kashi, Corn Flakes, All-Bran, Frosted Flakes, Rice Crispies, Special K, Raisin Bran, Bear Naked, Weight Watchers, Heartland |
| **D** | D+ | Post, Grape Nuts, Shredded Wheat |
| | D | |
| | D− | |
| **F** | F | Kraft, Nabisco, Back To Nature |

# CEREAL

**WHAT YOU NEED TO KNOW**

Currently, choosing a socially responsible cereal is one of the easiest ways to make a difference with your dollars. There are a wide variety of excellent choices available in most supermarkets.

**GREEN HERO**

## Nature's Path

☆ GAM certified Green Business
☆ Named one of Canada's Greenest Employers
☆ Sponsors environmental efforts and festivals

**CORPORATE VILLAIN**

## Back To Nature (Kraft)

☠ Part of #2 worst company on the earth[4]
☠ MM's "Worst Corporation" list for 5 years[38]
☠ Currently target of 2 major boycotts[16,40]
☠ Named global climate change laggard[10]

**RESOURCES**

🖳 www.naturespath.com
🖳 www.envirokidz.com
🖳 www.bobsredmill.com
🖳 www.alvaradostreetbakery.com

# CHIPS

| | | |
|---|---|---|
| **A** | **A+** | |
| | **A** | |
| | **A–** | Barbara's, Little Bear, Bearitos, Garden of Eatin', Hain, Terra |
| **B** | **B+** | Food Should Taste Good, Lundberg, Kettle Chips |
| | **B** | Lay's, Cheetos, Doritos, Fritos, Sun Chips, Tostitos, Ruffles, Quaker, Funyuns, Stacy's |
| | **B–** | Pepperidge Farm |
| **C** | **C+** | |
| | **C** | True North, Cape Cod, Solea, Dirty's, Eat Smart, Boulder, Glicks, Genisoy, Guiltless Gourmet, Utz, Hawaiian |
| | **C–** | Pringles, Mission, Pirate's Booty, Robert's American Gourmet |
| **D** | **D+** | |
| | **D** | French's |
| | **D–** | Alexia |
| **F** | **F** | Nabisco |

# CHIPS

**BUYING TIPS**
✓ Look for chips made with organic ingredients
✓ Avoid hydrogenated, saturated and trans fats
✓ Buy larger quantities to reduce packaging

**GREEN HERO**
## Kettle Chips

☆ 100% of waste oil turned into biodiesel
☆ Restored local wetlands habitat
☆ One of the largest solar arrays in NW
☆ Gives tons of potatoes to hunger orgs

**CORPORATE VILLAIN**
## Nabisco (Kraft)

☠ Greenwash Award for public deception[18]
☠ Named global climate change laggard[10]
☠ Currently target of 2 major boycotts[16,40]
☠ Paid $208 million to Washington lobbyists[8]

**RESOURCES**
🖳 www.barbarasbakery.com
🖳 lundberg.com
🖳 www.kettlefoods.com

# CHOCOLATE

| | | |
|---|---|---|
| **A** | A+ | Equal Exchange, Divine, AlterEco |
| | A | Shaman, Sjaak's, Coco-Zen, Theo, SweetRiot |
| | A– | Rapunzel, Endangered Species |
| **B** | B+ | Green & Black's, Ah!Laska, Terra Nostra, Lake Champlain, Newman's Own, Cloud Nine, Tropical Source, Sunspire, Dagoba |
| | B | |
| | B– | |
| **C** | C+ | Chocolove, Lindt, Ghirardelli |
| | C | Nutella, Ferrero Rocher, Droste, Russell Stover, Whitman's, Ritter |
| | C– | Godiva |
| **D** | D+ | |
| | D | Hershey's, Scharffen Berger |
| | D– | Swiss Miss |
| **F** | F | Nestle, Perugina, Toblerone, Mars, Ovaltine, Cadbury, Dove, M&M |

# CHOCOLATE

**WHAT YOU NEED TO KNOW**
Recently, the ILO, UNICEF and US State Department uncovered the widespread use of child slave labor in the chocolate industry — up to 40% of all chocolate is currently being produced in this way.

**BUYING TIPS**
✓ Companies in the A category are slave-free
✓ Look for chocolate that is fair trade certified
✓ Buy organic chocolate when available

**GREEN HERO**

## Equal Exchange

☆ GAM certified Green Business
☆ Business Ethics Award winner
☆ Industry leader in fair trade movement
☆ 4x Awarded "Most Democratic Workplace"

**CORPORATE VILLAIN**

## Nestle

☠ Aggressive takeovers of family farms[43]
☠ "Most Irresponsible" corporation award[3]
☠ Involved in child slavery lawsuit[43]
☠ Baby formula human rights boycott[36]

# CLEANING PRODUCTS

| | | |
|---|---|---|
| **A** | **A+** | Seventh Generation, Earth Friendly, Method, Ecover, Dr. Bronner's |
| | **A** | Biokleen, Planet, Air Therapy, ECOS, Citri-Glow, Citra-Solv |
| | **A–** | Mrs. Meyers |
| **B** | **B+** | LifeTree, Shaklee, Simple Green |
| | **B** | SC Johnson, Windex, Ziploc, Pledge, WD-40, Fantastik, Palmolive, Ajax, Drano, Vanish, Murphy's Oil, Glade |
| | **B–** | Mr. Bubble, Citrus Mate |
| **C** | **C+** | Bon Ami, 3M |
| | **C** | Hefty, Reynolds, Comet |
| | **C–** | |
| **D** | **D+** | Clorox, Green Works, Pine Sol, Tilex, SOS, Glad, Liquid-Plumr, Sara Lee, 409, Amway, Arm & Hammer |
| | **D** | Lysol, Easy-Off, Wizard, Chore Boy, Resolve, Woolite, Reckitt Benckiser |
| | **D–** | Soft Scrub, 20 Mule Team, Dial |
| **F** | **F** | Joy, Procter & Gamble, Ivory, Dawn, Swiffer, Mr. Clean, Febreze, Gain |

# CLEANING PRODUCTS

**BUYING TIPS**
✓ Look for non-petroleum based products
✓ Avoid products with chlorine/toxic chemicals

**GREEN HERO**
## Seventh Generation

☆ #1 best company on the planet
☆ Empowers consumers w/packaging
☆ Winner, Sustainability Report Award
☆ Socially Responsible Business Award

**GREEN HERO**
## Ecover

☆ GAM certified Green Business
☆ Winner, environmental leader award
☆ UN Global 500 Environment Honor Roll
☆ 1st truly ecological factory in the world

**CORPORATE VILLAIN**
## Clorox

☠ On MM's "10 Worst Corporations" list[38]
☠ Continues unnecessary animal testing[7]
☠ Refuses disclosure to consumers[9]
☠ Major producer of chlorine — dioxin[33]

# CLOTHING

| | | |
|---|---|---|
| **A** | A+ | Patagonia, Maggie's Organics, TS Designs, No Sweat Apparel |
| | A | No Enemy, Hempys, Ecolution, Deva, Justice Clothing, Autonomie |
| | A− | Levi's, Timberland, Eileen Fisher, American Apparel |
| **B** | B+ | Gap, Nordstrom, Liz Claiborne |
| | B | Cutter & Buck, Coldwater Creek |
| | B− | Eddie Bauer, Tommy Hilfiger, Abercrombie & Fitch, L.L. Bean |
| **C** | C+ | Nicole Miller, Burberry, Quiksilver, Rip Curl, Britannia, Gucci, Billabong |
| | C | Bass, Izod, Calvin Klein, PVH, H&M, North Face, American Eagle, J Crew |
| | C− | Men's Warehouse, Christian Dior |
| **D** | D+ | Beefy-T, Esprit, Ross, Guess, DKNY, Lands End, Champion, Hanes |
| | D | Bill Blass, Fruit of the Loom, Target, Express, Limited, Victoria's Secret, Perry Ellis, Saks, Lord & Taylor |
| | D− | TJ Maxx, Kohl's, JC Penney, Kmart |
| **F** | F | Wal-Mart, Sam's Club, Macy's, Polo, Marshall Fields, Foley's, Dillard's, Ralph Lauren, Consolidated, VF |

# CLOTHING

**WHAT YOU NEED TO KNOW**

The fact is that many of the clothes we wear today are made in sweatshops in the developing world. Better companies have either US-made clothing or strictly enforced human rights standards that ensure fair wages and safe working conditions.

**GREEN HERO**

## Maggie's Organics

☆ Socially Responsible Business Award
☆ Industry leader in fair trade movement
☆ (STAR) GAM "Top Rung", Ladder of Responsibility
☆ GAM certified Green Business

**CORPORATE VILLAIN**

## Macy's

☠ Weak code of conduct for sweatshops[9]
☠ RS "F" for overall social responsibility[43]
☠ Named "Sweatshop Laggard" by CEP[9]
☠ "Bottom Rung", Ladder of Responsibility[29]

**RESOURCES**

🖥 www.cleanclothes.org
🖥 www.americanapparel.net
🖥 www.maggiesorganics.com
🖥 www.patagonia.com

# COFFEE

| | | |
|---|---|---|
| **A** | **A+** | Cafe Campesino, Higher Grounds, Equal Exchange, Pura Vida, Grounds For Change, Peace Coffee, AlterEco, Dean's Beans |
| | **A** | Thanksgiving, Café Mam, Caffe Ibis, Larry's Beans, Alterra, Pachamama |
| | **A–** | Green Mountain, Newman's Own, LOCAL COFFEE SHOPS |
| **B** | **B+** | Starbucks, Seattle's Best |
| | **B** | |
| | **B–** | Millstone, Peet's |
| **C** | **C+** | |
| | **C** | Continental, Eight O'Clock, Hill Bros, MJB |
| | **C–** | Caribou, illy, LaVazza |
| **D** | **D+** | |
| | **D** | International Delight |
| | **D–** | |
| **F** | **F** | Maxwell House, Gevalia, Nescafe, Sanka, Folgers, Yuban, Nestle, Land O' Lakes, General Foods, CoffeeMate |

# COFFEE

**WHAT YOU NEED TO KNOW**
Global coffee prices have plummeted recently, pushing some coffee farmers in the developing world to the brink of starvation. Buying fair trade coffee is now more important than ever.

**BUYING TIPS**
✓ Look for fair trade, shade grown, organic
✓ Support local, independent coffee shops

**GREEN HERO**

## Grounds For Change

☆ B Lab Certified Responsible Company
☆ Industry leader in fair trade movement
☆ Fair trade, organic, shade grown coffee

**CORPORATE VILLAIN**

## Nescafe (Nestle)

☠ Involved in union busting outside US[43]
☠ "Bottom Rung", Ladder of Responsibility[29]
☠ Aggressive takeovers of family farms[43]
☠ Baby formula human rights boycott[36]

**RESOURCES**
🖥 www.transfairusa.org
🖥 www.groundsforchange.com
🖥 www.equalexchange.com

# COMPUTERS & ACCESSORIES

| | | |
|---|---|---|
| **A** | **A+** | |
| | **A** | GreenDisk |
| | **A−** | HP, Dell, Intel, Cisco, Google |
| **B** | **B+** | Apple, IBM |
| | **B** | Adobe, AMD, Lucent |
| | **B−** | Sony, Canon, NEC, Lexmark, Avaya |
| **C** | **C+** | Toshiba |
| | **C** | Brother, Imation, Novell, Oki, Asus, Fujitsu, Logitech, SanDisk, Seagate, Lenovo, Oracle, Kensington, 3COM, Epson, Fellowes, Creative, Best Buy, Plantronics |
| | **C−** | Sanyo, Sharp, Panasonic, Maxell, Belkin, LSI, NCR |
| **D** | **D+** | Micron, Philips, Samsung, JVC, Hitachi, Viewsonic |
| | **D** | LG, CompUSA |
| | **D−** | Acer, Gateway |
| **F** | **F** | Microsoft, GE |

# COMPUTERS & ACCESSORIES

**WHAT YOU NEED TO KNOW**

Computers have become an essential part of everyday life for many of us, but that need to stay up-to-date has also led to a rapidly growing problem of toxic computer waste in our landfills.

**GREEN HERO**

## HP (Hewlett Packard)

☆ Free return recycling of its computers
☆ Perfect 100 on HRC Equality Index
☆ Countless awards for business ethics

**CORPORATE VILLAIN**

## Microsoft

☠ RS "F" for overall social responsibility[29]
☠ Named "abusive monopoly" by US Court[36]
☠ Paid $98 million to Washington lobbyists[8]
☠ Greenpeace "Green Electronics Laggard"[33]
☠ Refuses disclosure on its business[9]

**RESOURCES**

💻 www.electronicstakeback.com
💻 www.svtc.org

# CONDIMENTS & DRESSINGS

| | | |
|---|---|---|
| **A** | **A+** | Eden, Annie's Naturals |
| | **A** | Sierra Nevada, Vegenaise, San-J |
| | **A–** | Woodstock Farms, Spectrum, Muir Glen, Hain, Hollywood, Westbrae, Organicville, Follow Your Heart |
| **B** | **B+** | Ginger People, Nasoya, OrganicVille, Bragg's, Newman's Own |
| | **B** | |
| | **B–** | Pepperidge Farms |
| **C** | **C+** | |
| | **C** | Saffola, Thai Kitchen, McCormick, Tabasco, Tapatio, Sriracha, Lawry's |
| | **C–** | Kikkoman, La Victoria, Mrs. Dash |
| **D** | **D+** | Del Monte, Contadina, Jack Daniel's, Lea & Perrins, Heinz, Hidden Valley, KC Masterpiece |
| | **D** | Hunt's, La Choy, Gulden's, French's, Cattlemen's |
| | **D–** | Marie Callendar's |
| **F** | **F** | Miracle Whip, Kraft, Bull's Eye, A1, Grey Poupon, Best Foods, Lizano, Knorr, Good Seasons, Wish-Bone |

# CONDIMENTS & DRESSINGS

**WHAT YOU NEED TO KNOW**
Whether you're looking for ketchup, mustard, mayonnaise, soy sauce or salad dressing, there are now socially responsible brands of each.

**BUYING TIPS**
✓ Choose organic condiments when available

**GREEN HERO**
## Annie's Naturals

☆ Supports organic, family farms
☆ Created environmental studies scholarship
☆ GAM certified Green Business
☆ Regularly donates products to nonprofits

**CORPORATE VILLAIN**
## Miracle Whip (Kraft)

☠ Named "Top 10 Greenwasher"[36]
☠ Paid $208 million to Washington lobbyists[8]
☠ Involved in document deletion cover-up[36]

**RESOURCES**
💻 www.annies.com
💻 www.edenfoods.com

# COOKIES & CRACKERS

| | | |
|---|---|---|
| **A** | **A+** | Mary's Gone Crackers, Annie's, Nature's Path, Lydia's Organics |
| | **A** | San-J |
| | **A−** | Barbara's, Hain, Immaculate, Health Valley, Earth's Best, Late July, Edward & Sons, Alternative Baking Co, Sun Flour Baking Co, O'Cocos, Nature's Choice, Doctor Kracker |
| **B** | **B+** | Newman's Own, Cascadian Farm, Lundberg |
| | **B** | Quaker, Mother's, Mi-del |
| | **B−** | Pepperidge Farm |
| **C** | **C+** | Keebler, Kashi, Famous Amos, Sunshine, Kellogg's |
| | **C** | Pamela's, LU, Archway, Mrs. Fields, Manishewitz, Ryvita, Wasa, Gille |
| | **C−** | Ry Krisp |
| **D** | **D+** | |
| | **D** | |
| | **D−** | |
| **F** | **F** | Back To Nature, Snackwell's, Nabisco, Red Oval, Dove |

# COOKIES & CRACKERS

**WHAT YOU NEED TO KNOW**
The socially responsible cookie industry has recently exploded, so there's no longer any need to feel guilty about reaching into the cookie jar.

**GREEN HERO**
## Nature's Path

☆ GAM certified Green Business
☆ Named one of Canada's Greenest Employers
☆ Sponsors environmental efforts and festivals

**CORPORATE VILLAIN**
## Nabisco (Kraft)

☠ Part of #2 worst company on the earth[4]
☠ Currently the target of 2 major boycotts[16,40]
☠ Spent over $208 million on lobbyists[8]
☠ Greenwash Award for public deception[36]

**RESOURCES**
⌨ www.lydiasorganics.com
⌨ www.annies.com
⌨ www.naturespath.com
⌨ www.marysgonecrackers.com

For more detailed data visit – www.betterworldshopper.org

# COSMETICS

| | | |
|---|---|---|
| **A** | **A+** | Pangea Organics, EO |
| | **A** | Aubrey, Zia, Kiss My Face, Colorganics |
| | **A−** | Aveda, Body Shop, Dr. Hauschka, Lush, BWC |
| **B** | **B+** | Nature's Gate, Ecco Bella, Avon, Gabriel, Herbs of Grace, Zuzu |
| | **B** | Avalon Organics |
| | **B−** | Estee Lauder |
| **C** | **C+** | Neutrogena, Johnson & Johnson, Aveeno, Desert Essence, Burt's Bees |
| | **C** | La Cross, Sally Hansen, Wet & Wild, Cutex, Bare Escentuals |
| | **C−** | Nivea |
| **D** | **D+** | Physician's Formula, Melaleuca |
| | **D** | L'Oreal, Maybeline, Mary Kay |
| | **D−** | |
| **F** | **F** | Dove, Revlon, Almay, Max Factor, Pond's, Olay, Covergirl |

# COSMETICS

**WHAT YOU NEED TO KNOW**

While some cosmetics companies still carry out tests on animals, many smaller companies now provide animal and eco-friendly alternatives.

**BUYING TIPS**

✓ Choose companies that don't test on animals
✓ Look for products with organic ingredients

**GREEN HERO**

## EO

☆ Products never tested on animals
☆ GAM certified Green Business
☆ B Lab Certified Responsible Company
☆ Containers made from recycled PET bottles

**CORPORATE VILLAIN**

## CoverGirl (Procter & Gamble)

☘ Continues unnecessary animal testing[7]
☘ "Bottom Rung", Ladder of Responsibility[29]
☘ MM's "Worst Corporation" list for 2 years[38]
☘ Spent over $46 million on lobbyists[8]

**RESOURCES**

🖥 www.eoproducts.com
🖥 www.caringconsumer.com

# DAIRY ALTERNATIVES

| | | |
|---|---|---|
| **A** | **A+** | Organic Valley, Nancy's, Eden |
| | **A** | Wildwood, WholeSoy, Hemp Bliss |
| | **A–** | Stonyfield Farm, Follow Your Heart, Pacific, Soy/Rice/Almond Dream, So Delicious, WestSoy, 8th Continent |
| **B** | **B+** | Good Karma |
| | **B** | Tofu/Vegan/Almond Rella, Soya Kaas, ZenSoy |
| | **B–** | Earth Balance |
| **C** | **C+** | |
| | **C** | Silk, Lisanatti, Soy Moon, Soyco, Soymage, Veggie/Rice Slice, Vitasoy |
| | **C–** | Tofutti, Galaxy Nutritional |
| **D** | **D+** | Blue Diamond |
| | **D** | |
| | **D–** | |
| **F** | **F** | International Delight, Cool Whip, Carnation |

# DAIRY ALTERNATIVES

**BUYING TIPS**
✓ Choose organic products when available
✓ Look for items with easily recycled containers

**GREEN HERO**
## Eden Foods

☆ Ranked #15 best company on the planet
☆ CEP's highest social responsibility score
☆ Top rated for its organic integrity

**GREEN HERO**
## Nancy's

☆ Largely solar powered workplace
☆ GAM certified Green Business
☆ 2x Socially Responsible Business Awards

**CORPORATE VILLAIN**
## Cool Whip (Kraft)

☠ Currently target of 2 major boycotts[16,40]
☠ Named global climate change laggard[10]
☠ #2 contributor to Washington lobbyists[8]
☠ Involved in document deletion cover-up[36]

# DAIRY PRODUCTS

| | | |
|---|---|---|
| **A** | **A+** | Organic Valley, Nancy's, Organic Pastures, Straus Family Creamery |
| | **A** | Redwood Hill |
| | **A–** | Wallaby, Helios, Stonyfield Farm, Brown Cow, Lifeway, Rachel's |
| **B** | **B+** | Clover Stornetta, Yoplait |
| | **B** | Cabot, Dannon |
| | **B–** | |
| **C** | **C+** | Lactaid |
| | **C** | Sargento, Precious, Pavel's, Kozy Shack, Cascade Fresh, Crystal, Mountain High, President, Rondele, Alouette, Athenos, Chavrie, Land O' Lakes, Kerrygold, Hood, Laughing Cow, Alpine Lace, Daisy, Horizon |
| | **C–** | Tillamook, Weight Watchers |
| **D** | **D+** | Sara Lee, Continental |
| | **D** | |
| | **D–** | Hunt's, Reddi-Wip |
| **F** | **F** | Jell-O, Kraft, Back to Nature, Nestle, Knudsen, Velveeta, Cracker Barrel, Philadephia Cream Cheese, Borden, Alta Dena |

# DAIRY PRODUCTS

**WHAT YOU NEED TO KNOW**
While large corporate farms are the norm for the dairy industry, many small, family farms are fighting back by going organic in order to survive.

**BUYING TIPS**
✓ Look for "No Hormones" and "No Antibiotics"
✓ Choose items made with organic ingredients

**GREEN HERO**

## Organic Valley

☆ Largest US cooperative of small, family farms
☆ Top rated for its organic integrity
☆ Multiple responsible business awards

**CORPORATE VILLAIN**

## Cracker Barrel (Kraft)

☠ Part of #2 worst company on the earth[4]
☠ Currently the target of 2 major boycotts[16,40]
☠ Greenwash Award for public deception[36]

**RESOURCES**
🖥 www.cornucopia.org
🖥 www.organicvalley.coop
🖥 www.strausfamilycreamery.com

# DENTAL CARE

| | | |
|---|---|---|
| **A** | **A+** | Preserve |
| | **A** | Kiss My Face, Auromere |
| | **A−** | Tom's of Maine, Ecodent, NOW, Xyliwhite, Fuchs |
| **B** | **B+** | Radius, Natural Dentist, Jason, Nature's Gate |
| | **B** | Colgate, Ultra Brite, Desert Essence, Weleda |
| | **B−** | |
| **C** | **C+** | Burt's Bees, Reach, Rembrandt, Johnson & Johnson, Listerine |
| | **C** | POH, GUM, ACT, Chattem |
| | **C−** | |
| **D** | **D+** | Arm & Hammer, Aim, Mentadent |
| | **D** | |
| | **D−** | |
| **F** | **F** | Aquafresh, Sensodyne, Pepsodent, Scope, Oral-B, Fixodent, Anbesol, Procter & Gamble, Polident, Crest, Poligrip, Abreva, GlaxoSmithKline |

# DENTAL CARE

**WHAT YOU NEED TO KNOW**
Smaller, environmentally friendly companies now offer increasingly popular alternatives to the dental products of larger, mainstream corporations.

**BUYING TIPS**
- ✓ Look for products made with recycled content
- ✓ Buy items with easily recycled packaging

**GREEN HERO**

## Preserve (Recycline)

- ☆ Environmental leader in industry
- ☆ Products from 100% recycled plastic
- ☆ Take-back recycling of all products

**CORPORATE VILLAIN**

## Crest (Procter & Gamble)

- ☠ GAM "Bottom Rung" Responsibility Rating[29]
- ☠ NRDC named "environmental laggard"[39]
- ☠ Paid $46 million to Washington lobbyists[8]

**RESOURCES**
- 🖳 www.recycline.com
- 🖳 www.kissmyface.com

# EGGS

| | | |
|---|---|---|
| **A** | **A+** | Organic Valley |
| | **A** | Organic Pastures, Vital Farms, Lazy 69, Alexandre Kids, Old Friends, St. John Family, Burroughs Family, Keedysville, Schultz, World's Best Eggs, Stony Brook Valley |
| | **A–** | |
| **B** | **B+** | Clover Organic, Born Free, Pete & Gerry's, Egg Innovations, Wilcox, Stiebrs, Giving Nature, Farmers Hen |
| | **B** | |
| | **B–** | Sauder's, Country Hen |
| **C** | **C+** | Eggland's Best, Horizon Organic, Judy's Family Farm, 4 Grain, Chino Valley, Farmer's Harvest, Glaum |
| | **C** | Gold Circle Farms, Land O'Lakes, Horizon Organic, Eggology |
| | **C–** | Nulaid, Decoster |
| **D** | **D+** | Lucerne |
| | **D** | |
| | **D–** | Egg Beaters |
| **F** | **F** | |

# EGGS

**WHAT YOU NEED TO KNOW**
Factory farming has made egg production today a cruel and environmentally damaging endeavor. Seek out smaller, more humane options.

**BUYING TIPS**
✓ Look for cage-free or free-range eggs
✓ Buy organic eggs whenever possible
✓ Seek out recycled paper-based packaging

**GREEN HERO**
## Organic Valley

☆ Small, family farmer-owned cooperative
☆ Gives 10% of profits to local community
☆ Humane animal treatment a priority

**CORPORATE VILLAIN**
## EggBeaters (ConAgra)

☠ Involved in major accounting scandal[49]
☠ 2nd largest E. coli meat recall in history[40]
☠ Many worker safety & health violations[43]

**RESOURCES**
🖥 www.organicvalley.coop

# ELECTRONICS

| A | A+ | |
|---|---|---|
| | A | |
| | A− | |
| B | B+ | Apple, Kodak |
| | B | Texas Instruments |
| | B− | Sony, Aiwa, Canon, Norelco |
| C | C+ | Toshiba, Minolta, Konica, Denon |
| | C | 3M, Conair, TDK, Apex, Magnavox, Eveready, Best Buy, Fuji, Kenwood, Grundig, Pentax, Koss, Plantronics, Nikon, Tivo, Rayovac, Sennheiser, Coby, Uniden, Olympus |
| | C− | RCA, Panasonic, Sharp, Polaroid, Maxell, Fry's, Thomson, Haier, Sanyo, Energizer, Garmin, Sylvania |
| D | D+ | Samsung, Philips, Bosch, Viewsonic, Radio Shack, JVC, Vizio, Hitachi |
| | D | LG |
| | D− | Amazon, Nintendo, Mitsubishi, Emerson |
| F | F | Microsoft, GE, Duracell, Daewoo |

# ELECTRONICS

**WHAT YOU NEED TO KNOW**
Our addiction to the latest electronics has
created a significant drain on our energy grid
(even when they're off!) as well as a major
recycling problem.

**BUYING TIPS**
✓ Look for electronics with Energy Star labels
✓ Buy rechargeable (NiMH) batteries
✓ Choose electronics that are recyclable

**GREEN HERO**

## Apple

☆ Takes back iPods & computers for recycling
☆ All computers are Energy Star certified
☆ Perfect 100 on HRC Equality Index for 7 years

**CORPORATE VILLAIN**

## GE (General Electric)

☠ MM's "Worst Corporation" list for 5 years[38]
☠ Responsible for 116 toxic Superfund sites[43]
☠ #1 contributor to Washington lobbyists[8]
☠ #13 of PERI 100 Most Toxic Air Polluters[42]

**RESOURCES**
🖳 www.electronicstakeback.com
🖳 www.svtc.org

# ENERGY BARS

| | | |
|---|---|---|
| **A** | **A+** | CLIF, Luna, Alpsnack, Optimum, Nature's Path |
| | **A** | BumbleBar, Nutiva |
| | **A–** | ReBar, Raw Revolution, Larabar, Health Valley, Think, Boomi, ProBar |
| **B** | **B+** | Kind, Crispy Cat, Cascadian Farm, Nature Valley, General Mills |
| | **B** | Quaker |
| | **B–** | |
| **C** | **C+** | |
| | **C** | Atkins, Roman Meal, Tiger's Milk, Soy Joy, Fit Smart, Promax, Met-Rx, Odwalla, Genisoy, Fubar, Sunbelt |
| | **C–** | Kellogg's, Kashi, Nutrigrain |
| **D** | **D+** | |
| | **D** | |
| | **D–** | Zone |
| **F** | **F** | Balance, South Beach, PowerBar, Kudos, Snickers, Slim Fast |

# ENERGY BARS

**WHAT YOU NEED TO KNOW**
Because many energy bar companies have truly stepped up to the plate, your choice of energy bar is one of the easiest ways to make a powerful difference for people and the planet.

**GREEN HERO**
## CLIF

☆ #10 best company on the earth
☆ Winner, Business Ethics Award
☆ EPA Green Power Leader award winner

**CORPORATE VILLAIN**
## Balance (Kraft)

☠ Part of #2 worst company on the earth[4]
☠ Named global climate change laggard[10]
☠ Named "Top 10 Greenwasher"[36]
☠ #2 contributor to Washington lobbyists[8]

**RESOURCES**
🖳 www.clifbar.com
🖳 www.alpsnack.com
🖳 www.bumblebar.com
🖳 nutiva.com

# ENERGY DRINKS

| | | |
|---|---|---|
| **A** | **A+** | Guayaki, CLIF, Adina |
| | **A** | Steaz, Sambazon |
| | **A–** | Honest Tea, Bossa Nova, Zola |
| **B** | **B+** | Monster, Starbucks, Hansen's, Blue Sky, Worx, Recharge |
| | **B** | Gatorade, SoBe, MDX, Propel, AMP |
| | **B–** | |
| **C** | **C+** | |
| | **C** | 5-Hour Energy, FRS, Red Bull, Rip It, Bawls, Atkins, Rockstar, Go Girl, Muscle Milk, Guru, Fubar, Everlast, Celsius, Met-Rx, Xenergy, Jones |
| | **C–** | Arizona, Snapple, Special K |
| **D** | **D+** | |
| | **D** | Lipton |
| | **D–** | Ensure |
| **F** | **F** | Boost, Slim Fast, Fuze, Vitamin Water, Full Throttle, Powerade, Vault, Glaceau, Tab, BPM |

# ENERGY DRINKS

**WHAT YOU NEED TO KNOW**
Just in the last 2 years have socially responsible choices for energy drinks finally become available. It's important to support these options wherever you find them.

**BUYING TIPS**
✓ Buy drinks in aluminum or glass containers

**GREEN HERO**
## Guayaki

☆ Organic, fair trade certified products
☆ Uses sustainably harvested, rainforest plants
☆ 3x Awarded "Most Democratic Workplace"
☆ GAM certified Green Business

**CORPORATE VILLAIN**
## Full Throttle (Coca Cola)

☠ MM's "Worst Corporation" list for 3 years[38]
☠ Hinders clean water access abroad[16]
☠ Target of major human rights boycotts[22]

**RESOURCES**
🖥 guayaki.com
🖥 www.steaz.com
🖥 www.stopcorporateabuse.org

# FAST FOOD & CASUAL DINING

| | | |
|---|---|---|
| **A** | A+ | |
| | A | Chipotle, Burgerville, Pizza Fusion, Evos, Boloco, Organic To Go |
| | A– | LarkBurger, Le Pan Quotidien |
| **B** | B+ | Bruegger's Bagels, Einstein Bros. |
| | B | In-N-Out, Noodles & Co |
| | B– | |
| **C** | C+ | Panera, Subway |
| | C | Church's Chicken, Dunkin Donuts, Togo's, Blimpie, Chuck E Cheese, Ruby Tuesdays, Applebee's, IHOP |
| | C– | Denny's, Red Lobster, Olive Garden, Red Robin, Popeye's, Papa John's, DQ, Quiznos, Macaroni Grill, Chik-fil-A, Little Caesar's, Panda Express |
| **D** | D+ | Jack in the Box, Qdoba, Carrabba's, Hardee's, Sonic, Boston Market, TGI Fridays, Outback Steak, Carl's Jr. |
| | D | Cracker Barrel, Domino's |
| | D– | Burger King, Wendy's, Arby's |
| **F** | F | KFC, Taco Bell, McDonald's, Pizza Hut, Long John Silver, Baja Fresh |

# FAST FOOD & CASUAL DINING

**WHAT YOU NEED TO KNOW**
The overall picture of the highly competitive fast food industry is not a pretty one, but if you find yourself in a pinch, there are a handful of companies to choose from that are on the cutting edge of responsibility. Support them whenever possible and let them know that you appreciate their efforts.

**GREEN HERO**
## Chipotle

☆ Actively sources from family farms
☆ 40% of beans utilized are organic
☆ 70% of meat utilized is natural-raised

**CORPORATE VILLAIN**
## KFC (Kentucky Fried Chicken)

☠ Linked to rainforest destruction abroad[33]
☠ Involved with plastic toy sweatshops[43]
☠ Target of major consumer boycott[22]
☠ Evidence of false nutritional claims[43]

**RESOURCES**
⌨ chipotle.com
⌨ www.burgerville.com

# FEMININE CARE

| | | |
|---|---|---|
| **A** | A+ | Seventh Generation |
| | A | Keeper, Moon Cup, Diva Cup, Gladrags |
| | A− | Maxim, Organic Essentials, Natracare |
| **B** | B+ | |
| | B | |
| | B− | Kotex, Poise |
| **C** | C+ | EPT, Stayfree, O.B., Carefree |
| | C | Summer's Eve, Clear Blue Easy, Vagisil |
| | C− | Playtex |
| **D** | D+ | First Response |
| | D | |
| | D− | |
| **F** | F | Always, Tampax, Massengill |

# FEMININE CARE

**WHAT YOU NEED TO KNOW**
Much of the effort for socially responsible business has been driven by women, so it's not surprising that there are many great options in this category.

**BUYING TIPS**
✓ Buy care products with less packaging waste

**GREEN HERO**
## Seventh Generation

☆ Ranked #1 best company on the planet
☆ Empowers consumers w/packaging
☆ Socially Responsible Business Award

**CORPORATE VILLAIN**
## Tampax (Procter & Gamble)

☠ MM's "Worst Corporation" list for 2 years[38]
☠ Continues unnecessary animal testing[7]
☠ Target of major consumer boycott[22]

**RESOURCES**
🖥 gladrags.com
🖥 www.keeper.com
🖥 www.seventhgeneration.com
🖥 www.divacup.com

# FROZEN DINNERS

| | | |
|---|---|---|
| **A** | A+ | |
| | A | Amy's Kitchen |
| | A– | Rising Moon, Moosewood, Applegate Farms, Cedarlane, Seeds of Change, Ethnic Gourmet, Organic Classics |
| **B** | B+ | Cascadian Farm, Linda McCartney |
| | B | Ian's, Totino's |
| | B– | |
| **C** | C+ | |
| | C | Foster Farms, Michelina's, Tony's, Red Baron, Claim Jumper, Michael Angelo's, Gorton's, Van de Kamps, Health Is Wealth, Ling Ling, White Castle, Lean Gourmet, Freschetta |
| | C– | Kashi, Quorn, Weight Watchers |
| **D** | D+ | Birds Eye, Swanson, Hungry Man, TGI Friday's, Ore-Ida, Smart Ones, Boston Market, Bagel Bites |
| | D | |
| | D– | Healthy Choice, Marie Callender's, Banquet, Alexia |
| **F** | F | Uncle Ben's, Boca, Lean Cuisine, Tyson, South Beach, Hot Pockets, Bertolli, Stouffer's |

# FROZEN DINNERS

**WHAT YOU NEED TO KNOW**
Today's stress-filled lifestyles have created increasing demand for quick and easy meals. Luckily, a number of responsible companies have decided to focus on options that are good for people and the planet.

**GREEN HERO**

## Amy's Kitchen

☆ Donates food to relief efforts
☆ Produces all-vegetarian, organic foods
☆ GAM certified Green Business

**CORPORATE VILLAIN**

## Stouffer's (Nestle)

☠ Baby formula human rights boycott[36]
☠ "Most Irresponsible" corporation award[3]
☠ Aggressive takeovers of family farms[43]
☠ Involved in union busting outside US[43]

**RESOURCES**
🖥 www.amyskitchen.com
🖥 www.risingmoon.com
🖥 www.seedsofchange.com

# FRUIT & VEGETABLES

| | | |
|---|---|---|
| **A** | **A+** | FARMERS MARKETS, CSAs |
| | **A** | Earthbound Farm, Sunridge Farms |
| | **A−** | Stahlbush, Cal-Organic, Bunny Luv, Woodstock Farms, Made In Nature, Grimmway Farms, Sunview, Sno Pac |
| **B** | **B+** | Cascadian Farm, HerbThyme, Pure Pacific, Green Giant, Newman's Own |
| | **B** | Driscoll's, Tropicana, Ian's |
| | **B−** | Ocean Spray, Sunsweet, Sun-Maid, Sunkist |
| **C** | **C+** | |
| | **C** | Ready Pac, Salad Time, Flav-R-Pac |
| | **C−** | |
| **D** | **D+** | Birds Eye, C&W, Ore-Ida, Del Monte, Hidden Valley |
| | **D** | Dole |
| | **D−** | Alexia, Fresh Express |
| **F** | **F** | |

# FRUIT & VEGETABLES

**WHAT YOU NEED TO KNOW**

Fresh produce is the vanguard of the organic foods movement. It's particularly important to buy local produce, so attend your local farmers' market or join a CSA (community supported agriculture) farm.

**BUYING TIPS**

✓ Buy organic, locally grown produce

**GREEN HERO**

## Earthbound Farm

☆ GAM certified Green Business
☆ Social Venture Network member
☆ Provider of 100% organic produce

**CORPORATE VILLAIN**

## Fresh Express (Chiquita)

☠ MM's "Worst Corporation" list for 2 years[38]
☠ Hired Columbian criminals to protect crops[36]
☠ EC overall responsibility rating of POOR[22]
☠ Evaded taxes using offshore bank accounts[43]

**RESOURCES**

🖳 www.localharvest.org

# GASOLINE

| | | |
|---|---|---|
| **A** | **A+** | |
| | **A** | |
| | **A–** | |
| **B** | **B+** | Sunoco |
| | **B** | Petro Canada |
| | **B–** | Hess |
| **C** | **C+** | Citgo |
| | **C** | Gulf, Sinclair, Husky, Mohawk, Irving, Royal Farms, Rutter's, Astro, Murphy, Pioneer, QuickChek, Wawa, Tesoro, QuikTrip, RaceTrac, Zephyr, Circle K, Costco |
| | **C–** | |
| **D** | **D+** | Valero, Diamond Shamrock, Beacon, Ultramar, Stop N Go, Total, Shamrock |
| | **D** | Marathon, Ashland, Speedway, SuperAmerica, Pilot, Flying J |
| | **D–** | BP, Arco, Shell, Conoco, Phillips 66, Jet, Superclean Tosco, Union 76 |
| **F** | **F** | Exxon, Mobil, Esso, Chevron, Texaco, Unocal |

# GASOLINE

**WHAT YOU NEED TO KNOW**

The petroleum industry is one of the least socially and environmentally responsible on the planet, so if you don't want to get your hands dirty, you should sell your car. For the rest of us, it's very important to avoid the companies at the bottom of this category as they are some of the most destructive in existence.

**BUYING TIPS**

✓ Locate the best ranked gas station near your home and work

**GREEN HERO**

## Sunoco

☆ Most eco-friendly refineries in industry
☆ Only oil signatory to CERES Principles
☆ 1st company to recognize global warming

**CORPORATE VILLAIN**

## Exxon-Mobil

☠ #1 worst corporation on the planet[4]
☠ Repeated violator of human rights[43]
☠ #5 in "Top 100 Corporate Criminals"[38]
☠ Paid $176 million to Washington lobbyists[8]
☠ Only Negative Score ever given by HRC[35]
☠ Extensive record of environmental damage[36]

# HAIR CARE

| | | |
|---|---|---|
| **A** | A+ | EO, Dr. Bronner's, Druide |
| | A | Aubrey Organics, Kiss My Face |
| | A– | Aveda, Tom's of Maine, Body Shop, Lush |
| **B** | B+ | Nature's Gate, Ecco Bella, Jason, Alba, Pure & Basic, Giovanni, Shikai, Paul Mitchell, Pure Essentials, BWC |
| | B | Avalon, Desert Essence, Emerald Forest, Aloe Vera 80 |
| | B– | |
| **C** | C+ | Neutrogena, Aveeno, Burt's Bees |
| | C | Citre Shine, Dep, Biosilk, AquaNet, Prell, Matrix, Joico, Biolage, Crew, Finesse, Rogaine |
| | C– | |
| **D** | D+ | L'Oréal, Pureology, White Rain, |
| | D | |
| | D– | Selsun Blue |
| **F** | F | Dove, Suave, Axe, SunSilk, Revlon, L.A. Looks, Herbal Essences, Pert, Pantene, Clairol, Aussie, Flex, Head & Shoulders, Nexxus, Tresemme, VO5, St. Ives, Infusium, Revlon |

# HAIR CARE

**BUYING TIPS**
✓ Avoid products tested on animals
✓ Seek out items made with organic ingredients
✓ Look for recyclable containers — #1, #2
  plastic
✓ Buy larger quantities to reduce packaging

**GREEN HERO**

## Druide

☆ 100% sustainably harvested ingredients
☆ Uses strict ECOCERT organic standards
☆ Fair trade, organic ingredients
☆ Industry leader in environment category

**CORPORATE VILLAIN**

## Clairol (Proctor & Gamble)

☠ Continues unnecessary animal testing[7]
☠ MM's "Worst Corporation" list for 2 years[38]
☠ GAM "Bottom Rung" Responsibility Rating[29]
☠ NRDC named "environmental laggard"[39]
☠ Paid $46 million to Washington lobbyists[8]

**RESOURCES**
🖳 www.druide.ca
🖳 www.aveda.com
🖳 www.thebodyshop.com
🖳 www.aubrey-organics.com

# HOTELS

| | | |
|---|---|---|
| **A** | A+ | |
| | A | Kimpton Hotels, Monaco, Palomar |
| | A− | |
| **B** | B+ | |
| | B | Marriott, Courtyard, Ritz Carlton, Renaissance, Bulgari |
| | B− | Saunders Hotel Group |
| **C** | C+ | Motel 6, Novotel, Sofitel, Westin, Red Roof Inn, Days Inn, Howard Johnson, Travelodge, Knights Inn, Wyndham, Super 8, Ramada, Hawthorn, Comfort Inn/Suites, Econo Lodge, Hyatt, Harrah's, Quality Inn, Clarion |
| | C | Best Western, Radisson |
| | C− | Sheraton, Westin, Starwood, MGM Mirage, Carlson, Holiday Inn |
| **D** | D+ | Hilton, Hampton Inn, DoubleTree, Embassy Suites, Conrad |
| | D | |
| | D− | |
| **F** | F | |

# HOTELS

**WHAT YOU NEED TO KNOW**
Whether for business or pleasure, choosing where you stay can have a greater impact than even how you travel there and back.

**BUYING TIPS**
✓ Whenever possible, stay in a locally-owned inn, bed & breakfast, or international hostel.

**GREEN HERO**

## Kimpton Hotels

☆ Environmental leader in the hotel industry
☆ Perfect 100 on HRC Equality Index
☆ Green Seal certified green lodging
☆ CAM certified Green Business

**CORPORATE VILLAIN**

## DoubleTree (Hilton)

☠ Rated "Very Poor" by Ethical Consumer[22]
☠ CC foot dragging on climate change efforts[14]
☠ Low score on HRC Equality Index[35]

**RESOURCES**
🖥 www.environmentallyfriendlyhotels.com
🖥 www.travelocity.com/greentravel

# ICE CREAM & FROZEN DESSERTS

| | | |
|---|---|---|
| **A** | **A+** | |
| | **A** | Sambazon, Wholesoy, Amy's Kitchen |
| | **A−** | Ben & Jerry's, Stonyfield Farm, So Delicious, Purely Decadent, Alden's, Rice/Soy Dream, Julie's Organic |
| **B** | **B+** | Newman's Own, FrutStix, Wholly Wholesome, Tru Whip, Ah!Laska, Starbucks, Pillsbury, Yoplait |
| | **B** | Cabot |
| | **B−** | Pepperidge Farm |
| **C** | **C+** | Dr. Oetker |
| | **C** | Crystal, Fruitfull, It's-It, Ciao Bella, Mrs. Smith's, Mrs. Fields, Hood |
| | **C−** | Tofutti, Weight Watchers, Godiva |
| **D** | **D+** | Sara Lee, Duncan Hines |
| | **D** | Dole, Hershey's |
| | **D−** | Marie Callendar's, Reddi-wip |
| **F** | **F** | Edy's, Dreyer's, Eskimo Pie, Nestle, Häagen Dazs, Skinny Cow, Breyer's, Dove, Klondike, Good Humor, Kraft, Cool Whip, Jell-O, Snickers |

# ICE CREAM & FROZEN DESSERTS

**BUYING TIPS**
✓ Choose ice cream with organic ingredients
✓ Look for fair trade coffee/chocolate flavors

**GREEN HERO**

## Sambazon

☆ Business Ethics award winner
☆ B Lab Certified Responsible Company
☆ Uses strict ECOCERT organic standards

**CORPORATE VILLAIN**

## Dreyer's (Nestle)

�># Baby formula human rights boycott[36]
�># "Most Irresponsible" corporation award[3]
�># Involved in child slavery lawsuit[43]
�># Aggressive takeovers of family farms[43]

**RESOURCES**
🖳 www.amys.com
🖳 www.sodeliciousdairyfree.com
🖳 www.wholesoyco.com
🖳 www.sambazon.com

# INSURANCE COMPANIES

| | | |
|---|---|---|
| **A** | A+ | Better World Club |
| | A | |
| | A– | |
| **B** | B+ | |
| | B | |
| | B– | Chubb, TIAA-CREF, Nationwide |
| **C** | C+ | Cigna, Aetna, Principal Financial, Progressive |
| | C | Travelers, Allstate, Pacific Life, Esurance, UnumProvident, USAA, AAA, Amica, Humana, MetLife, Mutual of Omaha, Capital One, Safeco |
| | C– | Kaiser Permanente, Prudential, Farmers, Northwestern Mutual, United Healthcare, American Family |
| **D** | D+ | State Farm, MassMutual, GEICO, New York Life |
| | D | AFLAC, Liberty Mutual |
| | D– | |
| **F** | F | Blue Cross / Blue Shield, AIG |

# INSURANCE COMPANIES

**WHAT YOU NEED TO KNOW**
Whether for your car, health, home or life, most of us need to buy insurance sooner or later. As we've discovered with the recent corporate bailouts, who we choose to do business with can have serious implications for our personal and national pocketbooks.

**GREEN HERO**

## Better World Club

☆ Social Venture Network member
☆ CAM certified Green Business
☆ Only insurance signatory to CERES Principles

**CORPORATE VILLAIN**

## AIG (American International Group)

☠ MM's "Worst Corporation" list for 2 years[38]
☠ Rated "Very Poor" by Ethical Consumer[22]
☠ Paid $78 million to Washington lobbyists[8]
☠ $170 billion paid by taxpayers to bailout[41]

**RESOURCES**
🖥 www.betterworldclub.com
🖥 www.jdpower.com/insurance

# JUICE

| | | |
|---|---|---|
| **A** | **A+** | Organic Valley, Adina |
| | **A** | Sambazon, Kombucha Botanica |
| | **A –** | Santa Cruz Organic, Purity, Kern's, Columbia Gorge, Zola, Happy Planet, Apple & Eve, Bossa Nova, Lakewood |
| **B** | **B+** | Ginger People, Cascadian Farm, Hansen's, Mountain Sun, Newman's Own, RW Knudsen, After the Fall |
| | **B** | Naked Juice, Tropicana, Gatorade |
| | **B –** | Sunkist, Ocean Spray, TreeTop, V8, Campbell's, Florida's Natural |
| **C** | **C +** | Biotta |
| | **C** | Odwalla, Sunny D, Horizon |
| | **C –** | ReaLemon, Snapple, Mott's, Sunny Delight, Welch's, Martinelli's, Jamba Juice, POM Wonderful |
| **D** | **D+** | Del Monte, Langers |
| | **D** | Dole |
| | **D –** | |
| **F** | **F** | Hawaiian Punch, Capri Sun, Libby's, Crystal Light, Minute Maid, Simply Orange, Juicy Juice, Back to Nature, Kool-Aid |

# JUICE

**BUYING TIPS**

✓ Purchase organic juices when available
✓ Buy juices in aluminum or glass containers
✓ #1 or #2 when plastics are the only option
✓ Buy larger quantities to reduce packaging

**GREEN HERO**

## Organic Valley

☆ Small family farmer-owned co-operative
☆ Gives 10% of profits to local community
☆ Humane animal treatment a priority
☆ Ranked #3 best company on the planet

**CORPORATE VILLAIN**

## Minute Maid (Coca Cola)

☠ MM's "Worst Corporation" list for 3 years[38]
☠ Hinders clean water access abroad[16]
☠ Target of major human rights boycotts[22]

**RESOURCES**

🖥 www.organicvalley.coop
🖥 www.kombuchabotanica.com
🖥 www.sambazon.com

# LAUNDRY SUPPLIES

| | | |
|---|---|---|
| **A** | **A+** | Seventh Generation, Earth Friendly, Oxo Brite, Method, Ecover |
| | **A** | Biokleen, Planet, Mountain Green, ECOS |
| | **A –** | Country Save, Bio Pac, Mrs. Meyers, Oasis |
| **B** | **B+** | Lifetree, Environne, Shaklee |
| | **B** | Fab, Fresh Start, Dynamo, Suavitel |
| | **B –** | Shout, Spot Shot |
| **C** | **C +** | |
| | **C** | |
| | **C –** | |
| **D** | **D+** | Arm & Hammer, Static Guard, All, Wisk, Sunlight, Surf, Snuggle, Sun, Cuddle Soft, Oxi Clean, Xtra, Clorox, Green Works |
| | **D** | Woolite, Calgon, Cling Free, Spray'n Wash, Vivid |
| | **D –** | Purex, 20 Mule Team Borax |
| **F** | **F** | Downy, Bounce, Era, Ivory, Febreze, Tide, Cheer, Biz, Bold, Gain, Dreft |

# LAUNDRY SUPPLIES

**BUYING TIPS**
✓ Avoid #3 plastic containers
✓ Choose #1 or #2 plastic when needed
✓ Avoid phosphates and chlorine bleach

**GREEN HERO**

## Ecover

☆ GAM certified Green Business
☆ Winner, environmental leader award
☆ UN Global 500 Environment Honor Roll
☆ 1st truly ecological factory in the world

**CORPORATE VILLAIN**

## Tide (Procter & Gamble)

☖ Continues unnecessary animal testing[7]
☖ MM's "Worst Corporation" list for 2 years[38]
☖ GAM "Bottom Rung" Responsibility Rating[29]
☖ NRDC named "environmental laggard"[39]
☖ Paid $46 million to Washington lobbyists[8]

**RESOURCES**
🖳 www.seventhgeneration.com
🖳 ecover.com
🖳 www.methodhome.com
🖳 www.planetinc.com
🖳 www.biokleenhome.com

# MEAT ALTERNATIVES

| | | |
|---|---|---|
| **A** | **A+** | |
| | **A** | Amy's Kitchen, Fantastic Foods, Wildwood, Sunshine Burgers, Local Tofu, Turtle Island, Tofurky |
| | **A−** | Small Planet, FarmSoy, Vermont Soy, Green Cuisine, Unisoy, Yves, TofuTown, Twin Oaks |
| **B** | **B+** | Nasoya, SoyBoy, Tofu Shop, Fresh Tofu, Sunergia, Central Soyfoods |
| | **B** | Ian's |
| | **B−** | |
| **C** | **C+** | Pete's Tofu, Gardenburger |
| | **C** | Mori-Nu, Vitasoy, White Wave, Soy Deli, Veat, Veggie Patch, Health Is Wealth, Sweet Earth, Primal Strips |
| | **C−** | Quorn, Morningstar Farms |
| **D** | **D+** | Full Circle |
| | **D** | |
| | **D−** | Lightlife |
| **F** | **F** | Boca |

# MEAT ALTERNATIVES

**WHAT YOU NEED TO KNOW**

Meat alternatives have come a long way since the days of tofu jokes. Burgers, hot dogs, chicken strips, lunch meat, and more are now convincingly tasty in vegetarian form and tend to have a smaller ecological footprint than their counterparts.

**GREEN HERO**

## Tofurky (Turtle Island)

☆ EPA Certified 100% Green Power
☆ Highest standards of organic integrity
☆ 1st food sponsor of The Humane Society

**CORPORATE VILLAIN**

## Boca (Kraft)

☠ Greenwash Award for public deception[36]
☠ MM's "Worst Corporation" list for 5 years[38]
☠ Named global climate change laggard[10]
☠ Paid $208 million to Washington lobbyists[8]

**RESOURCES**

🖥 www.amyskitchen.com
🖥 www.tofurky.com

# MEAT PRODUCTS

| | | |
|---|---|---|
| **A** | **A+** | Organic Prairie |
| | **A** | Lindner Bison, Green Zabiha |
| | **A–** | Shelton's, MBA Brand, Coleman, Niman Ranch, Diestel, Applegate Farms, Five Dot Ranch, Eel River |
| **B** | **B+** | |
| | **B** | |
| | **B–** | |
| **C** | **C+** | Empire Kosher |
| | **C** | Foster Farms, Valley Fresh, Saag's, Hickory Farms, Underwood |
| | **C–** | |
| **D** | **D+** | Sara Lee, Ball Park Franks, Hillshire Farm, Armour, Jimmy Dean, SPAM, Farmer John, Dinty Moore, Stagg, Jennie-O |
| | **D** | Perdue |
| | **D–** | Smithfield, Farmland, Eckrich, Slim Jim, Premium Standard, Hebrew National, Cook's, Banquet, Healthy Choice |
| **F** | **F** | Oscar Mayer, Louis Rich, Tyson, Butterball, Libby's |

# MEAT PRODUCTS

**WHAT YOU NEED TO KNOW**
Meat production tends to consume more resources than agriculture, so it's especially important to choose sustainable, humane options.

**BUYING TIPS**
✓ Choose free-range, organic meat options

**GREEN HERO**
## Organic Prairie (Organic Valley)

☆ Small, family farmer cooperative
☆ Gives 10% of profits to local community
☆ Humane animal treatment a priority

**CORPORATE VILLAIN**
## Tyson Foods

☠ MM's "Worst Corporation" list for 2 years[38]
☠ CEP "F" for overall social responsibility[9]
☠ Guilty of 20+ violations of Clean Air Act[43]
☠ #52 in "Top 100 Corporate Criminals"[38]

**RESOURCES**
🖳 www.organicprairie.com
🖳 www.smartchicken.com
🖳 www.colemannatural.com

# MEDICAL

| | | |
|---|---|---|
| **A** | **A+** | Traditional Medicinals |
| | **A** | |
| | **A–** | Nature's Way |
| **B** | **B+** | Ricola |
| | **B** | Medtronic, Baxter Intl |
| | **B–** | Novo Nordisk |
| **C** | **C+** | Johnson & Johnson, McNeil, Band-Aid, Rolaids, Neosporin, Visine, 3M, Benadryl, Tylenol, Bengay, Motrin |
| | **C** | Chattem, Genentech, Halls, Unisom, Cortizone, Kaopectate, Biovail |
| | **C–** | Del, Mead Johnson, AstraZeneca |
| **D** | **D+** | Schering-Plough, PhRMA, Tyco, Bristol-Myers Squibb, WR Grace |
| | **D** | Reckitt Benckiser, Bausch & Lomb, Novartis, Eli Lilly, Sanofi-Aventis |
| | **D–** | Merck, Abbott, Amgen |
| **F** | **F** | Alka-Seltzer, Q-Tips, Tums, Unilever, Bayer, GlaxoSmithKline, Vaseline, Procter & Gamble, Wyeth, Roche, Pfizer, Pharmacia, Pepto-Bismol, Metamucil, Robitussin, Whitehall-Robins, Day/Nyquil, Advil, Vick's |

# MEDICAL

**WHAT YOU NEED TO KNOW**
Pharmaceutical companies are some of the most powerful and least responsible of any on the planet. When you do have a choice of medical products, it is very important that you choose the better companies.

**BUYING TIPS**
✓ Make sure to look on the back of the box to see what company manufactures an item

**GREEN HERO**

## Traditional Medicinals

☆ GAM certified Green Business
☆ Powered by 100% renewable energy
☆ Utilizes sustainable harvesting of wild herbs
☆ Organic, fair trade, biodynamic ingredients

**CORPORATE VILLAIN**

## Pfizer

�909 MM's "Worst Corporation" list for 5 years[38]
☣ Named "Environmental Laggard" by CEP[9]
☣ #17 in "Top 100 Corporate Criminals"[38]
☣ Paid $126 million to Washington lobbyists[8]
☣ #41 of PERI 100 Most Toxic Air Polluters[42]

# MILK & ALTERNATIVES

| | | |
|---|---|---|
| **A** | **A+** | Eden Foods, Organic Valley, Straus Family, Organic Pastures, Nancy's |
| | **A** | Wildwood, Hemp Bliss |
| | **A−** | Stonyfield Farm, Pacific, WestSoy, Rice/Soy/Almond Dream, Helios, 8th Continent, So Delicious, Lifeway |
| **B** | **B+** | Clover Stornetta, Living Harvest |
| | **B** | Zensoy, Almond Breeze |
| | **B−** | Smart/Earth Balance |
| **C** | **C+** | Lactaid |
| | **C** | Land O' Lakes, Crystal, Kikkoman, Milkman, Horizon Organic, Organic Cow, Hood, Vitasoy, Silk |
| | **C−** | |
| **D** | **D+** | Blue Diamond |
| | **D** | |
| | **D−** | |
| **F** | **F** | Knudsen, Nestle, Alta Dena, Borden, Garelick, Berkeley Farms, Meadow Gold, Mayfield, Dairy Ease |

# MILK & ALTERNATIVES

**WHAT YOU NEED TO KNOW**
Now there are a wide range of socially responsible options for both dairy and non-dairy milk lovers.

**GREEN HERO**
## Organic Valley

☆ Ranked #3 best company on the planet
☆ Small, family farmer-owned co-operative
☆ Humane animal treatment a priority
☆ Gives 10% of profits to local community

**GREEN HERO**
## Straus Family

☆ 1st 100% organic dairy in US
☆ Uses returnable glass bottles for milk
☆ Utilizes methane capture for waste
☆ Small, sustainable family farm

**RESOURCES**
🖥 www.organicvalley.coop
🖥 www.strausmilk.com
🖥 www.edenfoods.com
🖥 www.cornucopia.org

# OFFICE & SCHOOL SUPPLIES

| | | |
|---|---|---|
| **A** | **A +** | Seeds Green Printing |
| | **A** | ReBinder, The Green Office, HP, GreenerPrinter |
| | **A –** | Herman Miller, Xerox |
| **B** | **B +** | IBM |
| | **B** | Office Depot, Staples, Ricoh |
| | **B –** | Canon, Pitney Bowes |
| **C** | **C +** | 3M, Scotch, Post-it, Hallmark, Bic, Crayola, Parker, Shaeffer |
| | **C** | DHL, Imation, US Post Office, Ikon, Olympus, Henkel, Epson, Papermate, Rubbermaid, Sanford, Sharpie, Uni-ball, Expo, Zebra, Brother, Fiskars, Elmer's, WB Mason, Pentel, Duck, Fellowes, Pilot, Kensington, Smead |
| | **C –** | Airborne Express |
| **D** | **D +** | FedEx, BASF, OfficeMax, UPS |
| | **D** | Avery |
| | **D –** | Mead, Trapper Keeper, At-A-Glance, Day Runner, Cambridge, Columbian, Five Star, Smurfit |
| **F** | **F** | |

# OFFICE & SCHOOL SUPPLIES

**WHAT YOU NEED TO KNOW**

Many of the items we use during the day are in some way related to our workplace. If you have any potential influence over office purchasing, consider suggesting a shift in funds over to more socially responsible products.

**GREEN HERO**

## Herman Miller

✫ 100 Most Ethical Companies list, 7 years
✫ Business Ethics Award, 2 time winner
✫ Perfect 100 on HRC Equality Index
✫ Winner of Social Capitalist Award for ethics

**CORPORATE VILLAIN**

## Day Runner (MeadWestvaco)

☠ Named global climate change laggard[14]
☠ Refuses disclosure to consumers[9]
☠ Continues unnecessary animal testing[7]
☠ CEP "F" for overall social responsibility[9]

**RESOURCES**

🖥 www.rebinder.com
🖥 www.thegreenoffice.com
🖥 seedsgreenprinting.com

# OIL, VINEGAR, OLIVES & PICKLES

| | | |
|---|---|---|
| **A** | **A+** | Eden Foods, Annie's, Canaan Fair Trade, AlterEco |
| | **A** | Nutiva |
| | **A–** | Napa Valley, Bionaturae, NOW, Hain, Rapunzel, Spectrum, Hollywood |
| **B** | **B+** | Bragg's, Natural Value, Marukan, Republic of Tea, Newman's Own, Cascadian Farm, Santa Barbara |
| | **B** | |
| | **B–** | Smart/Earth Balance |
| **C** | **C+** | |
| | **C** | Star, Canola Harvest, Saffola, Sagra, Nakano, Lindsay, Minasso, Cains, Nathan's, Armstrong |
| | **C–** | Mezzetta, Mt. Olive, B&G |
| **D** | **D+** | Heinz, Del Monte, Vlasic |
| | **D** | |
| | **D–** | Wesson, Pam |
| **F** | **F** | Mazola, Claussen, Crisco, Bertolli |

# OIL, VINEGAR, OLIVES & PICKLES

**WHAT YOU NEED TO KNOW**
A number of socially responsible companies now offer conventional and organic oils and vinegars.

**BUYING TIPS**
✓ Choose organic oil, vinegar & cooking spray

**GREEN HERO**
## Canaan Fair Trade

☆ GAM certified Green Business
☆ Produces the only fair trade certified olives
☆ Supports Palestinian farmers & communities

**CORPORATE VILLAIN**
## Pam (ConAgra)

☠ 2nd largest E. coli meat recall in history[40]
☠ #50 in "Top 100 Corporate Criminals"[38]
☠ Ceres "Climate Change Laggard"[10]

**RESOURCES**
🖥 www.canaanfairtrade.com
🖥 www.edenfoods.com
🖥 altereco.com

# ONLINE

| | | |
|---|---|---|
| **A** | **A+** | |
| | **A** | Ethical Ocean, Etsy, Care2, Mozilla, Firefox, Craigslist, Wikipedia, Better World Books, Change, GoodGuide |
| | **A–** | Google, Chrome, YouTube |
| **B** | **B+** | Apple, Safari |
| | **B** | |
| | **B–** | SquareSpace, Orbitz |
| **C** | **C+** | hulu, Groupon |
| | **C** | eBay, Expedia, Priceline, MySpace, Facebook, LinkedIn, Qwest, Twitter, Blogspot, WordPress, Cablevision |
| | **C–** | EarthLink, Blizzard, DoubleClick |
| **D** | **D+** | Flickr, Cox |
| | **D** | AOL |
| | **D–** | Amazon, IMDb, Yahoo!, Charter, AT&T |
| **F** | **F** | Comcast, Road Runner, Microsoft, Internet Explorer, MSN, Bing, Live, Time Warner |

# ONLINE

**WHAT YOU NEED TO KNOW**
In the information age, what ISP and browser you use is just as important as where you browse. Whenever possible, support those companies and organizations that turn some of your dollars (and clicks) into making a difference on and offline.

**BUYING TIPS**
✓ Buy local, used items online when possible
✓ Support open source and community efforts

**GREEN HERO**
## Google

☆ 100 Most Ethical Companies list, 3 years
☆ Industry leader in fighting climate change
☆ Perfect 100 on HRC Equality Index, 4 years

**CORPORATE VILLAIN**
## Bing (Microsoft)

☠ CEP "F" for overall social responsibility[9]
☠ Paid $98 million to Washington lobbyists[8]
☠ EC overall responsibility rating of POOR[22]

**RESOURCES**
⌨ www.ethicalocean.com
⌨ www.etsy.com

# OUTDOOR GEAR

|   |     |                                                                                      |
|---|-----|--------------------------------------------------------------------------------------|
| **A** | **A+** | Patagonia                                                                        |
|   | **A**  | Teva, GoLite, Klean Kanteen, Gaiam                                                |
|   | **A−** | Timberland                                                                        |
| **B** | **B+** |                                                                                  |
|   | **B**  | REI, Mountain Equipment Co-op, prAna, SIGG                                        |
|   | **B−** | Kelty, Sierra Designs, LL Bean, Eddie Bauer, Chaco                                |
| **C** | **C+** | TomTom                                                                            |
|   | **C**  | Columbia, Marmot, Keen, Coleman, Royal Robbins, North Face, Nalgene, Eagle Creek, CamelBak |
|   | **C−** | Garmin, Merrell                                                                   |
| **D** | **D+** | LuluLemon, Dick's Sporting Goods                                                  |
|   | **D**  |                                                                                  |
|   | **D−** |                                                                                  |
| **F** | **F**  | Jansport, Eastpak, Reef                                                           |

# OUTDOOR GEAR

**WHAT YOU NEED TO KNOW**
While enjoying the outdoors, make certain that the equipment you use is preserving the natural environment rather than helping to destroy it.

**GREEN HERO**
## Timberland

☆ Business Ethics Award winner
☆ 4x Named World's Most Ethical Company
☆ Labelling leader, eco-social footprint
☆ EPA Green Power Award winner

**GREEN HERO**
## Patagonia

☆ Environmental leader in industry
☆ Plastic bottles recycling pioneer — fleece
☆ 1% of sales goes to enviro groups
☆ Powered by 100% renewable energy

**CORPORATE VILLAIN**
## Jansport (Vanity Fair)

☠ "Bottom Rung", Ladder of Responsibility[29]
☠ Low score on HRC Equality Index[35]
☠ Refuses disclosure to consumers[9]
☠ EC responsibility rating of VERY POOR[22]
☠ Named global climate change laggard[14]

For more detailed data visit – www.betterworldshopper.org

# PAPER & PAPER PRODUCTS

| A | A+ | New Leaf, Seventh Generation, Earth Friendly, Green Forest |
| | A | Greenline, Living Tree, Sugarmade |
| | A− | Cascades |
| B | B+ | IBM, Xerox, HP, Tork, Natural Value |
| | B | Mohawk, Staples, Office Depot, Marcal |
| | B− | Canon, Scotties, Kleenex, Viva, Scott, Cottonelle, Purely Cotton |
| C | C+ | 3M, Post-It, Weyerhaeuser |
| | C | Brother, Epson, Smead, WB Mason |
| | C− | Wausau |
| D | D+ | FedEx, OfficeMax, Boise, Domtar |
| | D | Hammermill, International Paper, Avery |
| | D− | Mead, Cambridge |
| F | F | Georgia-Pacific, Quilted Northern, Angel Soft, Dixie, Brawny, Sparkle, Soft n' Gentle, Vanity Fair, Zee, Mardi Gras, Softly, Bounty, Puffs, Charmin, Ultra, Envision |

# PAPER & PAPER PRODUCTS

**WHAT YOU NEED TO KNOW**
Just remember one thing: PAPER = TREES.

**BUYING TIPS**
✓ Look for post-consumer recycled content
✓ Choose non-chlorine bleached paper options

**GREEN HERO**
## New Leaf

☆ Forest Stewardship Council certified
☆ Offers 100% post-consumer options
☆ Invented the Eco-Audit for books, etc.
☆ Uses sustainably harvested wood

**CORPORATE VILLAIN**
## Georgia-Pacific (Koch)

☠ #44 in "Top 100 Corporate Criminals"[38]
☠ GP gives lowest environmental ranking[33]
☠ #41 of PERI 100 Most Toxic Air Polluters[42]
☠ Paid $66 million to Washington lobbyists[8]
☠ EC responsibility rating of VERY POOR[22]

**RESOURCES**
🖥 newleafpaper.com
🖥 www.seventhgeneration.com

# PASTA & SAUCE

| | | |
|---|---|---|
| **A** | **A+** | Eden Foods, Annie's |
| | **A** | Amy's Kitchen |
| | **A–** | Muir Glen, DeBoles, Simply Organic, Walnut Acres, Rising Moon, Garden Time, Bionaturae, Seeds of Change |
| **B** | **B+** | Lundberg, Newman's Own, Hodgson Mill, Natural Value, Betty Crocker, Progresso |
| | **B** | Golden Grain, Pasta Roni |
| | **B–** | Prego, Campbell's |
| **C** | **C+** | |
| | **C** | Barilla, Ronzoni, Stella, McCormick, Emeril's, American Beauty, Emilia, Halbrand, De Cecco, Prince, Goya, New World Pasta, Manischewitz, DaVinci, Lawry's |
| | **C–** | Mezzetta |
| **D** | **D+** | Contadina, Classico, Del Monte |
| | **D** | |
| | **D–** | Chef Boyardee, Hunt's |
| **F** | **F** | Kraft, Buitoni, Back To Nature, Ragu, Bertolli, Knorr |

# PASTA & SAUCE

**BUYING TIPS**
✓ Look for items made with organic ingredients
✓ Buy larger quantities to reduce packaging

**GREEN HERO**
## Eden Foods

☆ Ranked #15 best company on the planet
☆ CEP's highest social responsibility score
☆ GAM certified Green Business

**GREEN HERO**
## Lundberg

☆ Uses 100% renewable energy in production
☆ Uses organic, sustainable farming practices
☆ No animal testing of its products
☆ Top award for treatment of employees

**CORPORATE VILLAIN**
## Back To Nature (Kraft)

☿ #2 contributor to Washington lobbyists[8]
☿ Currently the target of 2 major boycotts[16,40]
☿ Greenwash Award for public deception[36]
☿ Part of #2 worst company on the earth[4]

**RESOURCES**
🖥 www.edenfoods.com
🖥 lundberg.com

# PEANUT BUTTER & JELLY

| | | |
|---|---|---|
| **A** | **A+** | |
| | **A** | |
| | **A−** | Rapunzel, Woodstock Farms, Santa Cruz Organic, Crofter's, Bionaturae, Maranatha, Arrowhead Mills, Seeds of Change |
| **B** | **B+** | Cascadian Farm, Kettle Foods |
| | **B** | |
| | **B−** | Smart/Earth Balance, Smuckers, Jif, Goober, Laura Scudder's, Simply Fruit |
| **C** | **C+** | |
| | **C** | Nutella, Joyva, Robertson's, Sorrell Ridge, Glick's, Teddie, Adams, Bonne Maman, Manischewitz, Knott's |
| | **C−** | Welch's |
| **D** | **D+** | |
| | **D** | |
| | **D−** | Peter Pan |
| **F** | **F** | Skippy |

# PEANUT BUTTER & JELLY

**BUYING TIPS**
✓ Look for items made with organic ingredients
✓ Buy larger quantities to reduce packaging

**GREEN HERO**
## Rapunzel

☆ Fair trade & organic leader in food ind.
☆ Supports global sustainable farming
☆ Produced 1st 100% organic chocolate

**GREEN HERO**
## Kettle Foods

☆ 100% of waste oil turned into biodiesel
☆ Restored local wetlands habitat
☆ One of the largest solar arrays in Northwest
☆ Gives tons of potatoes to hunger orgs

**CORPORATE VILLAIN**
## Peter Pan (ConAgra)

☠ #50 in "Top 100 Corporate Criminals"[38]
☠ Ceres "Climate Change Laggard"[10]
☠ 2nd largest E. coli meat recall in history[40]
☠ Many worker safety & health violations[43]

# PET CARE

| | | |
|---|---|---|
| **A** | **A+** | BioBag, Only Natural Pet Store |
| | **A** | Swheat Scoop, V-Dog, Honest Kitchen |
| | **A−** | Health Valley, Feline Pine, Karma, Natural Life, Raw Advantage |
| **B** | **B+** | PetGuard, Newman's Own, Halo, Dr. Harvey's, Artemis |
| | **B** | Heartland, Zuke's, Sensible Choice, Avoderm, Canidae, Happy Dog |
| | **B−** | PETCO, Natural Balance |
| **C** | **C+** | Castor & Pollux, Back to Basics |
| | **C** | PetSmart, Jonny Cat, Nylabone, Breeder's Choice, Innova, Hartz, PhD, Old Mother Hubbard, EVO |
| | **C−** | Wellness |
| **D** | **D+** | Fresh Step, Scoop Away, Kibbles 'n Bits, Pounce, Meow Mix, Milk Bone, Blue Buffalo, Science Diet, 9 Lives |
| | **D** | Capstar, Arm & Hammer |
| | **D−** | Frontline, Heartgard |
| **F** | **F** | Advantage/tix, Revolution, Nutro, Fancy Feast, Gourmet, IAMS, Sheba, Tidy Cats, Dog Chow, Purina, Royal Canin, Alpo, ONE, Friskies, Whiskas, Eukanuba, Tender Vittles, Pedigree |

# PET CARE

**WHAT YOU NEED TO KNOW**
Recent innovations have been made in the area
of socially responsible pet care, so you should
have a number of excellent options to choose
from.

**BUYING TIPS**
✓ Buy pet food made with organic ingredients
✓ Buy cat litter made from renewable sources

**GREEN HERO**
## BioBag

☆ 100% biodegradable, corn-based material
☆ 100% compostable w/multiple certifications
☆ GAM certified Green Business

**CORPORATE VILLAIN**
## Purina (Nestle)

♟ "Most Irresponsible" corporation award[3]
♟ Involved in child slavery lawsuit[43]
♟ Aggressive takeovers of family farms[43]

**RESOURCES**
🖥 v-dog.com
🖥 www.onlynaturalpet.com
🖥 www.swheatscoop.com

# POPCORN, NUTS, PRETZELS & MIXES

| | | |
|---|---|---|
| **A** | **A+** | Equal Exchange, Eden |
| | **A** | |
| | **A–** | Arrowhead Mills, Woodstock Farms, Hain, Bearitos, Little Bear |
| **B** | **B+** | Newman's Own, Lesser Evil, Aurora Natural, Gardetto's, Chex Mix, Glad Corn, NOW, Food Should Taste Good |
| | **B** | Smartfood, Cracker Jack, Rold Gold, True North |
| | **B–** | |
| **C** | **C+** | |
| | **C** | Jolly Time, ExpresSnacks, Yaya's, Sahale, Pretzel Crisps |
| | **C–** | Pirate's Booty, Snyder's of Hanover |
| **D** | **D+** | Pop Secret, Emerald, Blue Diamond |
| | **D** | |
| | **D–** | Act II, Crunch 'n Munch, Jiffy Pop, Orville Redenbacher, Fiddle Faddle, David, Poppycock, Almond Accents |
| **F** | **F** | Planters, Corn Nuts, Back to Nature |

# POPCORN, NUTS, PRETZELS & MIXES

**WHAT YOU NEED TO KNOW**
When you're settling in to watch a little TV or a movie, what you put in that bowl next to the couch makes a big difference for the planet.

**GREEN HERO**
## Eden Foods

☆ Ranked #15 best company on the planet
☆ CEP's highest social responsibility score
☆ GAM certified Green Business

**GREEN HERO**
## Equal Exchange

☆ GAM certified Green Business
☆ Business Ethics Award winner
☆ Industry leader in fair trade movement

**CORPORATE VILLAIN**
## Planters (Kraft)

�609 Part of #2 worst company on the earth[4]
�609 Currently the target of 2 major boycotts[16,40]
�609 #2 contributor to Washington lobbyists[8]

**RESOURCES**
⌨ www.equalexchange.coop

For more detailed data visit – www.betterworldshopper.org

# RETAIL STORES

| | | |
|---|---|---|
| **A** | **A+** | Patagonia |
| | **A** | |
| | **A–** | Timberland |
| **B** | **B+** | Nordstrom, Marks & Spencer |
| | **B** | REI, IKEA, Ace Hardware |
| | **B–** | L.L. Bean, Eddie Bauer |
| **C** | **C+** | |
| | **C** | Dollar General, The North Face, Neiman Marcus, Best Buy |
| | **C–** | Talbot's |
| **D** | **D+** | Bed Bath & Beyond, Dick's, Ross |
| | **D** | Target, BJ's, Saks Fifth Avenue, Home Depot, Kohl's |
| | **D–** | CVS, Osco, Save-On, Long's Drugs, JC Penney, Marshalls, Lowe's, Rite Aid |
| **F** | **F** | Wal-Mart, Sam's Club, Sears, Kmart, Big Lots, Orchard Supply Hardware, Land's End, Walgreens, Dillard's, Costco, Bloomingdale's, Macy's |

# RETAIL STORES

**GREEN HERO**

## Patagonia

☆ Environmental leader in industry
☆ Plastic bottles recycling pioneer — fleece
☆ 1% of sales goes to enviro groups
☆ Powered by 100% renewable energy

**GREEN HERO**

## Timberland

☆ Business Ethics Award winner
☆ 4x Named World's Most Ethical Company
☆ Labelling leader, eco-social footprint
☆ EPA Green Power Award winner

**CORPORATE VILLAIN**

## Walmart

☠ #3 worst company on the planet[4]
☠ CEP "F" for overall social responsibility[9]
☠ Sex-discrimination class-action lawsuit[36]
☠ Documented exploitation of child labor[43]
☠ Paid $41 million to Washington lobbyists[8]
☠ RS rated worst responsibility in industry[43]

**RESOURCES**

🖳 www.patagonia.com
🖳 www.timberland.com

# RICE & OTHER GRAINS

| | | |
|---|---|---|
| **A** | **A +** | Eden, AlterEco, Canaan Fair Trade |
| | **A** | Fantastic Foods |
| | **A –** | Near East, Seeds Of Change, Casbah |
| **B** | **B +** | Lundberg, Annie Chun's, Betty Crocker |
| | **B** | Rice-A-Roni, Quaker |
| | **B –** | Hungry Jack |
| **C** | **C +** | |
| | **C** | Minute Rice, Dynasty, Carolina, Mrs Cubbison's, Mahatma, McCormick, Success Rice, Goya, Manischewitz |
| | **C –** | |
| **D** | **D +** | Lipton, S&W, Hormel |
| | **D** | |
| | **D –** | |
| **F** | **F** | Kraft, Uncle Ben's, Knorr |

# RICE & OTHER GRAINS

**BUYING TIPS**
✓ Look for organic grains
✓ Buy in bulk to reduce packaging waste

**GREEN HERO**
## AlterEco
☆ Produces a range of 100% fair trade goods
☆ Works directly with local farmer cooperatives
☆ GAM certified Green Business
☆ Fair trade consumer education leader

**GREEN HERO**
## Canaan Fair Trade
☆ GAM certified Green Business
☆ Leader in fair trade integrity standards
☆ Supports Palestinian farmers & communities

**CORPORATE VILLAIN**
## Uncle Ben's (Mars)
☠ CEP "F" for overall social responsibility[9]
☠ On MM's "10 Worst Corporations" list[38]
☠ Evidence of involvement in child slave labor[43]
☠ Target of international fair trade campaign[18]
☠ "Bottom Rung", Ladder of Responsibility[29]

# SALSA, SPREADS & DIPS

|   | A+ | |
|---|---|---|
| **A** | A | Emerald Valley, Wildwood, Amy's, Fantastic Foods |
| | A− | Walnut Acres, Bearitos, Casbah, Rising Moon, Seeds Of Change, Muir Glen, Simply Organic |
| **B** | B+ | Newman's Own, Old El Paso |
| | B | Tostitos, Lay's, Fritos, Sabra |
| | B− | Pace |
| **C** | C+ | |
| | C | Nonna Lena's, Salpica, Frontera, La Victoria, Raquel's, Gringo, Micaelas, Green Mountain, Laura Scudder's, Cedar's, Litehouse, Haig's, Ortega, Native, Margaritaville, Mrs. Renfros |
| | C− | |
| **D** | D+ | Lipton, Chi Chi's |
| | D | |
| | D− | Rosarita |
| **F** | F | Taco Bell, Kraft |

# SALSA, SPREADS & DIPS

**WHAT YOU NEED TO KNOW**
This category includes everything from hummus to salsa to bean dip, and there are responsible choices to be had for every one.

**GREEN HERO**
## Amy's Kitchen

☆ Donates food to relief efforts
☆ Produces all-vegetarian, organic foods
☆ GAM certified Green Business

**GREEN HERO**
## Emerald Valley

☆ Socially Responsible Business Award
☆ 1% to humanitarian & ecological causes
☆ Green Business Of The Year Award

**CORPORATE VILLAIN**
## Taco Bell (Kraft)

☠ Named "Top 10 Greenwasher"[36]
☠ Involved in document deletion cover-up[36]
☠ MM's "Worst Corporation" list for 5 years[38]
☠ Paid $208 million to Washington lobbyists[8]

# SEAFOOD I

| | | |
|---|---|---|
| **A** | **A+** | Henry & Lisa's, EcoFish |
| | **A** | Wildcatch, Wild Planet, VitalChoice, Pelican's Choice, Wild Pacific |
| | **A−** | Blue Horizon Organic, RainCoast |
| **B** | **B+** | Whole Foods*, Nugget Market* |
| | **B** | Safeway*, Von's*, Pak N Save*, Bela, Contessa, Omega |
| | **B−** | Wegmans*, Target*, Harris Teeter* |
| **C** | **C+** | Ahold*, Giant*, Stop & Shop* |
| | **C** | Aldi*, Delhaize*, Walmart*, Sam's Club*, A&P*, Bumble Bee, Flott, Deep Sea, King Oscar, Beach Cliff, Van de Kamp's, Geisha, Ola!, Snow's, Vince's, Star, Swanson, Louis Kemp |
| | **C−** | Gorton's, Costco*, Price Chopper*, Giant Eagle*, Trader Joe's*, HEB* |
| **D** | **D+** | Kroger*, Food 4 Less*, Quik Stop*, King Soopers*, Ralph's*, Chicken of the Sea, Crown Prince, Starkist |
| | **D** | Meijer* |
| | **D−** | Cub Foods*, Albertson's*, Shaw's*, Lucky*, Sav A Lot*, Osco*, Jewel* |
| **F** | **F** | Publix*, Winn-Dixie* |

# SEAFOOD I

**WHAT YOU NEED TO KNOW**
One of the most important changes you can make is in choosing ecologically responsible seafood. Supermarkets are rated here solely based on the sustainability of their seafood selection and are noted with an asterisk.

**BUYING TIPS**
✓ Look for sustainable fishing labels
✓ Local freshwater is often a good choice
✓ See next section for more seafood guidance

**GREEN HERO**

## Henry & Lisa's

☆ Only environmentally sustainable fishing
☆ Conservation scientists advisory board
☆ Result of marine conservation groups

**GREEN HERO**

## Wildcatch

☆ Certified by Marine Stewardship Council
☆ Harvests only sustainable, wild seafood
☆ Works with nonprofits like Salmon Nation

**RESOURCES**
🖳 ecofish.com

# SEAFOOD II

| | | |
|---|---|---|
| **A** | A | Wild Alaskan Salmon, Arctic Char, Mackerel, Striped Bass, Mussels, Dungeness Crab, Trout, Wahoo, Sea Urchin, Barramundi, Pacific Halibut |
| **B** | B | Catfish, Stone Crab, Prawns, Clams, Oysters, Scallops, Squid, Black Cod, Sablefish, Sardines, Walleye, Pollock |
| **C** | C | Yellowtail, Snow/Blue Crab, Pacific Cod, Lobster, Herring, Smelt, Pacific Salmon, Tilapia, Mahi Mahi, Shrimp, Haddock, Crayfish, Whitefish, most Tuna, Red Porgy, Bluefish, Hake |
| **D** | D | King Crab, Flounder, Grouper, Sea Bass, Marlin, Monkfish, Sturgeon, Snapper, Sole, Swordfish, Rockfish, Caviar, Atlantic Cod, Turbot, Plaice, |
| **F** | F | Orange Roughy, Perch, Oreos, Shark, Atlantic Halibut, Farmed & Atlantic Salmon, Bluefin Tuna, Octopus, Eel, Skate, Tautog, Shad, Dogfish, Cobia |

# SEAFOOD II

**WHAT YOU NEED TO KNOW**
Our current fishing practices are destroying
ocean life at an unprecedented rate. Rather
than ranking companies, the chart to the left
shows which species are being more sustainably harvested and which are being fished out
of existence based on a synthesis of available
data from the three major organizations researching this issue: Environmental Defense
Fund, Monterey Bay Aquarium & Blue Ocean Institute. It also takes into account the
environmental costs of harvesting each kind
of seafood. Use it both at the supermarket
seafood counter and when you go out to eat.

**BUYING TIPS**
✓ When it's unclear, ask the deli staffer or server
   for more specifics about the fish
✓ When A or B category seafood is not available, consider non-seafood alternatives

**RESOURCES**
🖥 www.seafoodwatch.org
🖥 www.edf.org/seafood
🖥 www.blueocean.org/seafoods
🖥 www.msc.org

# SHOES

| | | |
|---|---|---|
| **A** | **A+** | Dansko, Blackspot, Patagonia, Autonomie Project |
| | **A** | Teva, Simple Shoes, Sole Rebels |
| | **A−** | Timberland, Birkenstock, Earth Shoes |
| **B** | **B+** | Zappos, Red Wing |
| | **B** | |
| | **B−** | Chaco |
| **C** | **C+** | Reebok, Nike, DMX, Rockport |
| | **C** | Ecco, Salomon, North Face, Crocs, Keen, UGG, DC |
| | **C−** | Adidas, Umbro, Ellesse, HI-TEC, Merrell |
| **D** | **D+** | New Balance, Stride Rite, Brooks, Lotto, FILA, K-Swiss, Keds, Sperry, Tommy Hilfiger |
| | **D** | Pentland, Puma |
| | **D−** | Skechers, Mizuno, Converse, ASICS, Saucony, Florsheim, Foot Locker, Nunn Bush |
| **F** | **F** | LA Gear, Vans, Reef, DISCOUNT & DEPARTMENT STORE BRANDS |

# SHOES

**WHAT YOU NEED TO KNOW**

Almost all store-bought shoes are made in factories in the developing world. The real question is: how are the workers treated, are they safe, and do they make enough of a wage to live decently? Your choices here will determine the answers to those questions for tens of thousands of families.

**GREEN HERO**

## Dansko

☆ GAM certified Green Business
☆ Powered by 100% renewable energy
☆ LEED Gold eco-certified main office

**CORPORATE VILLAIN**

## LA Gear

☠ Named "Sweatshop Laggard"[9]
☠ CEP "F" for overall social responsibility[9]
☠ Weak supplier code of conduct for workers[9]

**RESOURCES**

🖳 www.solerebelsfootwear.co
🖳 www.blackspotsneaker.org
🖳 www.dansko.com
🖳 www.autonomieproject.com

# SOAP

| | | |
|---|---|---|
| **A** | **A+** | Dr. Bronner's, Pangea Organics, EO, Method, Canaan Fair Trade |
| | **A** | Juniper Ridge, Aubrey, Kiss My Face, Auromere, Oregon Soap Co. |
| | **A–** | Tom's of Maine, Body Shop |
| **B** | **B+** | Jäsön, Sappo Hill, River Soap, Alba, Zum Bar, Nature's Gate, Plantlife, Shikai, Earth Therapeutics, Moon Valley, One With Nature, HUGO |
| | **B** | Avalon, Irish Spring, Softsoap, Palmolive, Tender Care |
| | **B–** | Clearly Natural |
| **C** | **C+** | Burt's Bees, Aveeno, Purell |
| | **C** | Germ-X, St. Ives, Pure & Natural, Coast, Olivella |
| | **C–** | Nivea, Coastal |
| **D** | **D+** | |
| | **D** | |
| | **D–** | Dial, Tone |
| **F** | **F** | Ivory, Safeguard, Olay, Zest, Gillette, Old Spice, Lava, Dove, Lever 2000, Caress, Axe, Suave |

# SOAP

**BUYING TIPS**
✓ Choose soaps that aren't tested on animals
✓ Buy soaps with less or recyclable packaging

**GREEN HERO**
## Dr. Bronner's

☆ Leader in organic standards integrity
☆ 5:1 CEO to worker salary cap
☆ Profits donated to variety of causes
☆ Liquid soaps in 100% recycled plastic
☆ Does not test on animals

**GREEN HERO**
## Pangea Organics

☆ GAM certified Green Business
☆ Never tests on ingredients on animals
☆ 2x Award Winner for Business Ethics

**CORPORATE VILLAIN**
## Dial

☠ Continues unnecessary animal testing[7]
☠ CEP "F" for overall social responsibility[9]
☠ Sexual discrimination/harassment suits[43]
☠ Refuses disclosure to consumers[9]

# SODA

| | | |
|---|---|---|
| **A** | **A+** | |
| | **A** | Steaz, Maine Root |
| | **A –** | Chill, Oogave, Sipp |
| **B** | **B+** | Santa Cruz Organic, Hansen's, Blue Sky, Newman's Own, RW Knudsen |
| | **B** | Izze, Sierra Mist, Tropicana, Mug, Pepsi, Slice, Mountain Dew |
| | **B –** | |
| **C** | **C +** | |
| | **C** | Bundaberg, Thomas Kemper, Faygo, Boylan, Bawls, Moxie, Reed's, China Cola, Shasta, Jolt, Virgil's, Jones, The Switch |
| | **C –** | Orangina, 7-Up, Snapple, A&W, Diet Rite, Squirt, Sunkist, Welch's, IBC, Stewart's, Dr Pepper, Canada Dry, Crush, RC Cola, Hires, Polar, Crystal Geyser, Weight Watchers, Arizona |
| **D** | **D +** | Henry Weinhard's |
| | **D** | |
| | **D –** | |
| **F** | **F** | Coca-Cola, Sprite, Fanta, Pibb Xtra, Barq's, Minute Maid, San Pellegrino, Fresca, Tab, Lipton |

# SODA

**WHAT YOU NEED TO KNOW**

If you're like most people, soda is a daily part of your diet. Move up on the responsible soda chain to avoid companies that are wrecking the planet.

**BUYING TIPS**

✓ Buy soda in aluminum or glass containers

**GREEN HERO**

## Steaz

☆ Organic drinks industry leader
☆ Profits donated to Sri Lankan village
☆ Supports sustainable farming practices
☆ Offers fair trade certified sodas

**CORPORATE VILLAIN**

## Coca-Cola

☠ MM's "Worst Corporation" list for 3 years[38]
☠ Hinders clean water access abroad[16]
☠ Target of major human rights boycotts[22]

**RESOURCES**

🖳 www.steaz.com
🖳 maineroot.com
🖳 www.oogave.com

# SOUPS, NOODLES & CURRIES

| | | |
|---|---|---|
| **A** | **A+** | Eden Foods, Annie's |
| | **A** | Amy's Kitchen, Fantastic Foods |
| | **A–** | Rapunzel, Walnut Acres, Imagine, Native Forest, Casbah, Nile Spice, Health Valley, Organic Planet, Seeds of Change, Shelton's, Muir Glen, Pacific Natural, Edward & Sons |
| **B** | **B+** | Progresso, Annie Chun's, Nasoya, Dr. McDougall's, Spice Hunter |
| | **B** | |
| | **B–** | Campbell's, Wolfgang Puck |
| **C** | **C+** | |
| | **C** | Thai Kitchen, Bear Creek, Swanson, Maruchan, Nissin, Tasty Bite, Sun Luck, Alessi, Snow's, Bar Harbor |
| | **C–** | |
| **D** | **D+** | Mrs. Grass, Herb Ox |
| | **D** | |
| | **D–** | Healthy Choice |
| **F** | **F** | Knorr, Lipton, Cup-A-Soup |

# SOUPS, NOODLES & CURRIES

**WHAT YOU NEED TO KNOW**
Whether it's instant noodles or pea soup, there are many excellent choices for hot, steaming, socially responsible meals.

**BUYING TIPS**
✓ Look for soups made with organic
  ingredients

**GREEN HERO**

## Rapunzel

☆ Fair trade & organic leader in food ind.
☆ Supports global sustainable farming
☆ Produced 1st 100% organic chocolate

**CORPORATE VILLAIN**

## Healthy Choice (ConAgra)

☠ MM's "Worst Corporation" list for 2 years[38]
☠ #50 in "Top 100 Corporate Criminals"[38]
☠ Ceres "Climate Change Laggard"[10]

**RESOURCES**
🖥 www.rapunzel.de/uk/
🖥 www.fantasticfoods.com
🖥 www.amyskitchen.com

# SUGAR, SPICES & SWEETENERS

| | | |
|---|---|---|
| **A** | **A+** | Wholesome Sweeteners, Eden Foods, AlterEco, King Arthur, Canaan Fair Trade, Equal Exchange, Frontier |
| | **A** | Simply Organic, Silk Road, Coombs, Great Northern |
| | **A−** | NOW, Hain, Florida Crystals, Spicely |
| **B** | **B+** | Spice Hunter, Lundberg, Bragg's |
| | **B** | |
| | **B−** | |
| **C** | **C+** | Splenda |
| | **C** | C&H, Domino, Sweet 'N Low, Butter Buds, McCormick, Sugar in the Raw, Spike, Morton, Goya, Lawry's, Adolph's |
| | **C−** | Spice Islands |
| **D** | **D+** | Hormel, Mrs. Butterworth's |
| | **D** | |
| | **D−** | Equal, Nutrasweet |
| **F** | **F** | Sugar Twin, Mrs. Dash, Molly McButter |

# SUGAR, SPICES & SWEETENERS

**WHAT YOU NEED TO KNOW**
Many of these items we buy once and keep using for years. If you want to make a difference while saving your budget, start here.

**BUYING TIPS**
✓ Buy in bulk to reduce packaging waste

**GREEN HERO**
## Wholesome Sweeteners

☆ 1st US fair trade certified sugar available
☆ Actively supports sustainable farming
☆ Makes a full line of organic sweeteners

**CORPORATE VILLAIN**
## Sugar Twin (Unilever)

☠ Continues unnecessary animal testing[7]
☠ EC responsibility rating of VERY POOR[22]
☠ Illegal toxic waste dumping abroad[36]

**RESOURCES**
🖥 www.wholesomesweeteners.com
🖥 www.frontiercoop.com
🖥 www.alterecofoods.com

# SUPERMARKETS

| | | |
|---|---|---|
| **A** | **A+** | FOOD CO-OPS, FARMERS MARKETS |
| | **A** | Whole Foods |
| | **A-** | |
| **B** | **B+** | Trader Joe's |
| | **B** | Wegmans, Nugget, Raley's |
| | **B-** | |
| **C** | **C+** | Fresh & Easy, Food Lion, Harris Teeter |
| | **C** | A&P, Fry's, Delhaize, Pathmark |
| | **C-** | Giant Eagle, Hannaford, ShopRite, Price Chopper, Price Mart, Shop N Save, ThriftWay, Weis, C&S, BJ's |
| **D** | **D+** | H.E.B., Roundy's, Aldi, Target, Von's, Pak 'n' Save, Safeway, Stop & Shop, Giant, Peapod |
| | **D** | |
| | **D-** | Long's, Osco, Meijer, Rite Aid, CVS |
| **F** | **F** | Walmart, Ralph's, Food 4 Less, QFC, Fred Meyer, King Soopers, Kroger, Kwik Shop, Quick Stop, Loaf N Jug, Winn-Dixie, Albertsons, Cub, Acme, Bigg's, Lucky's, Save-A-Lot, Shaw's, Star, Publix, Costco, Walgreens |

# SUPERMARKETS

**WHAT YOU NEED TO KNOW**
If you have a choice, changing where you shop is an incredibly powerful action that will support people and the planet above profit.

**GREEN HERO**
## Whole Foods

☆ BE's "Best Corporations" list for 3 years
☆ Powered by 100% renewable energy
☆ Business Ethics Award winner
☆ Established animal & poverty foundation
☆ Created animal compassion standards
☆ Leader in sourcing sustainable seafood

**CORPORATE VILLAIN**
## Walmart

�># MM's "Worst Corporation" list for 3 years[38]
�># Major toxic waste dumping fines[18]
�># #3 worst company on the planet[4]
�># CEP "F" for overall social responsibility[9]
�># Documented exploitation of child labor[43]
�># Paid $41 million to Washington lobbyists[8]

**RESOURCES**
🖳 www.localharvest.org
🖳 www.cooperativegrocer.coop

# TEA

| | | |
|---|---|---|
| **A** | **A+** | Numi, Equal Exchange, Guayaki, Eco Teas, Traditional Medicinals, Choice |
| | **A** | Zhena's Gypsy, Tulsi, Organic India, Rishi, Sencha, Oregon Chai, Leaf Spa, Arbor, Art of Tea, Davidson's |
| | **A–** | Honest Tea, Yogi, Kopali Organics, Tao Of Tea, Celestial Seasonings |
| **B** | **B+** | Sweet Leaf, Pacific Natural, Jones, Bionaturae, Newman's Own |
| | **B** | Pixie Mate, Tejava |
| | **B–** | Tazo, Republic Of Tea |
| **C** | **C+** | Bigelow |
| | **C** | Stash, Mighty Leaf, Harney & Sons, Triple Leaf, Coffee Bean & Tea Leaf |
| | **C–** | Arizona, Ito En, Twinings, Snapple, Red Rose |
| **D** | **D+** | Tetley, Good Earth |
| | **D** | |
| | **D–** | |
| **F** | **F** | Nestea, Lipton, PG Tips |

# TEA

**WHAT YOU NEED TO KNOW**
If you drink tea, you have an incredible selection of human and planet friendly varieties to pick from.

**BUYING TIPS**
✓ Look first for the fair trade label, then move on to organic, sustainably harvested, etc.

**GREEN HERO**
## Numi

☆ GAM certified Green Business
☆ Member of the Social Venture Network
☆ Socially Responsible Business Award

**GREEN HERO**
## Equal Exchange

☆ GAM certified Green Business
☆ Business Ethics Award winner
☆ Industry leader in fair trade movement

**CORPORATE VILLAIN**
## Nestea (Nestle)

☠ Involved in child slavery lawsuit[43]
☠ Aggressive takeovers of family farms[43]
☠ Involved in union busting outside US[43]
☠ "Most Irresponsible" corporation award[3]

# TOYS & GAMES

| | | |
|---|---|---|
| **A** | **A+** | |
| | **A** | Hazelnut Kids, Down to Earth Toys, Eco Toy Town |
| | **A−** | Wild Planet, Tree Hollow |
| **B** | **B+** | Mac |
| | **B** | |
| | **B−** | Sony, Playstation, Hot Wheels, Mattel |
| **C** | **C+** | Electronic Arts, Crayola |
| | **C** | Fisher Price, Wham-O, Lego, Sega, Namco, Ubisoft, Square Enix |
| | **C−** | GameStop, Blizzard, Activision, Warner Brothers |
| **D** | **D+** | Toys R Us, Babies R Us, Kids R Us |
| | **D** | |
| | **D−** | Nintendo, Wii, Wizards of the Coast, Disney, Playskool, Hasbro, Parker Brothers, Milton Bradley, Play-Doh, Nerf, Tonka, Transformers |
| **F** | **F** | Microsoft, Xbox, PC |

# TOYS & GAMES

## WHAT YOU NEED TO KNOW

The irresponsible manufacturing of toys and games does not always directly threaten us or our children, but it always endangers people or the environment in some part of the world.

## BUYING TIPS

✓ Look for less common, cooperative games
✓ Buy used toys & games when available
✓ Seek out shareware & open source games

## CORPORATE VILLAIN

### Tonka (Hasbro)

☠ Low score on HRC Equality Index[35]
☠ Named "Sweatshop Laggard" by CEP[9]
☠ Weak code of conduct for factories abroad[9]

## CORPORATE VILLAIN

### Xbox (Microsoft)

☠ Named "abusive monopoly" by US Court[36]
☠ Paid $98 million to Washington lobbyists[8]
☠ Greenpeace "Green Electronics Laggard"[33]
☠ Refuses disclosure on its business[9]

## RESOURCES

🖥 www.wildplanet.com
🖥 seriousgames.org

# VITAMINS

| | | |
|---|---|---|
| **A** | **A+** | |
| | **A** | New Chapter Organics, Deva |
| | **A−** | NOW Foods, Oregon's Wild Harvest, Spectrum |
| **B** | **B+** | Rainbow Light |
| | **B** | Nature's Way |
| | **B−** | Nutribiotic |
| **C** | **C+** | Sundown Naturals, Viactiv |
| | **C** | Nature's Life, Solaray, VegiLife, All One, GNC, Natrol, SuperNutrition, Solgar, Nature Made, Emergen-C, Jarrow, Carlson, Twinlab, Nature's Plus, Nature's Bounty, Weil, Source Naturals, Country Life, Wellesse |
| | **C−** | |
| **D** | **D+** | |
| | **D** | |
| | **D−** | |
| **F** | **F** | One-A-Day, Flinstones, Bayer, Centrum |

# VITAMINS

**BUYING TIPS**
✓ Look for organic ingredients in supplements
✓ Buy in recyclable bottles: #1, #2, or glass
✓ Purchase in bulk to reduce packaging waste

**GREEN HERO**

## New Chapter Organics

☆ Organic, sustainable, harvesting practices
☆ International biodynamic certification
☆ Extensive environmental awards
☆ Promotes efforts to sustain biodiversity

**GREEN HERO**

## NOW

☆ Reduced waste by 50% in 3 years
☆ Donates to WWF & Second Harvest
☆ Environmental & Sustainability Awards
☆ Industry leader in recycling efforts

**CORPORATE VILLAIN**

## Centrum (Pfizer)

☠ #41 of PERI 100 Most Toxic Air Polluters[42]
☠ #17 in "Top 100 Corporate Criminals"[38]
☠ MM's "Worst Corporation" list for 4 years[38]
☠ Paid $126 million to Washington lobbyists[8]

# WATER

| | | |
|---|---|---|
| **A** | **A+** | TAP / FILTERED |
| | **A** | |
| | **A–** | Earth Water . |
| **B** | **B+** | Ethos, Balance |
| | **B** | Propel, Aquafina, SoBe, Voss |
| | **B–** | Evian, Volvic, Dannon |
| **C** | **C+** | K2O |
| | **C** | La Croix, Hawaii, Ice Age, Icelandic Glacial, Fiji, Penta, Trinity, Essentia, Crystal Springs, Sparkletts, Metro Mint, Adirondack, Saratoga |
| | **C–** | Schweppes, Snapple, Crystal Geyser, Deja Blue, Arizona, Fruit2O |
| **D** | **D+** | |
| | **D** | |
| | **D–** | |
| **F** | **F** | Glaceau, Vitamin Water, Arrowhead, Smart Water, Dasani, Vittel, Perrier, Deer Park, Calistoga, S. Pellegrino, Vittel, Poland Spring, Zephyr Hills, Ozarka, Ice Mountain, Acqua Panna |

# WATER

**BUYING TIPS**
✓ Carry your own reusable bottle
✓ Buy fewer, larger bottles, and refill them
✓ ALWAYS recycle the bottles when done

**GREEN HERO**
## Earth Water

☆ 100% of profits donated to UNHCR
☆ Biodegradable water bottle

**CORPORATE VILLAIN**
## Arrowhead (Nestle)

☠ Baby formula human rights boycott[36]
☠ "Most Irresponsible" corporation award[3]
☠ Involved in child slavery lawsuit[43]

**CORPORATE VILLAIN**
## Dasani (Coca Cola)

☠ MM's "Worst Corporation" list for 3 years[38]
☠ Hinders clean water access abroad[16]
☠ Target of major human rights boycotts[22]

**RESOURCES**
🖥 www.earthgroup.org
🖥 www.ethoswater.com

# WINE

| | | |
|---|---|---|
| **A** | **A+** | LOCAL VINEYARDS |
| | **A** | Frey, Fetzer, La Rocca, Frog's Leap |
| | **A−** | Honeyrun, Kunde Estate, Alma Rosa |
| **B** | **B+** | Banrock Station, Rodney Strong, Sobon Estate, St. Francis, Bota Box |
| | **B** | Mountain Meadows, Cline, Kendall Jackson, French Rabbit, Benziger |
| | **B−** | Sutter Home, Alma Rosa |
| **C** | **C+** | Franzia, Lindemans, Turning Leaf, Ecco Domani, Luna di Luna |
| | **C** | Almaden, Jacob's Creek, Glen Ellen, Columbia Crest, Bogle, Inglenook, Delicato, Woodbridge |
| | **C−** | Dom Perignon, Krug, Bonny Doon, Beringer, Mondavi, Sterling, Cloudy Bay, Blossom Hill, Corbett Canyon |
| **D** | **D+** | Charles Shaw, Barefoot, Yellow Tail, Gallo, Korbel, Carlo Rossi, Andre |
| | **D** | |
| | **D−** | |
| **F** | **F** | Stag's Leap, Chateau Ste Michelle |

# WINE

**BUYING TIPS**
✓ Look for organic wine varieties on the shelf
✓ Support local vineyards — try their wine
✓ Buy in bulk to reduce packaging waste

**GREEN HERO**

## Fetzer

☆ Powered by 100% renewable energy
☆ All vineyards certified organic
☆ Reduced production waste by 94%
☆ Bottles are 40% recycled glass
☆ BE Award for Environmental Excellence

**GREEN HERO**

## Frey

☆ GAM certified Green Business
☆ Oldest organic US winery
☆ 1st US biodynamic wine producer

**RESOURCES**
🖥 www.fetzer.com
🖥 freywine.com
🖥 frogsleap.com
🖥 laroccavineyards.com
🖥 honeyrunwinery.com
🖥 www.kunde.com
🖥 almarosawinery.com

# PRODUCT CATEGORY INDEX

| CAN'T FIND... | LOOK UNDER... |
|---|---|
| Antiperspirant | Body Care |
| Apple Sauce | Canned Fruits & Vegetables |
| Bandages | Medical |
| Barbeque Sauce | Condiments & Dressings |
| Batteries | Electronics |
| Beans | Canned Beans, Chili & Stews |
| Bottled Water | Water |
| Bouillon | Soup, Noodles & Curries |
| Chicken | Meat Products |
| Cocoa | Chocolate |
| Cold Remedies | Medical |
| Corn Meal | Baked Goods & Baking Supplies |
| Couscous | Rice & Other Grains |
| Cottage Cheese | Dairy Products |
| Cough Drops | Medical |
| Crackers | Cookies & Crackers |
| Cream Cheese | Dairy Products |
| Creamer | Coffee |
| Credit Cards | Banks & Credit Cards |

| | |
|---|---|
| Mayonnaise | Condiments & Dressings |
| Mobile Phones | Cell Phones & Service |
| Mouthwash | Dental Care |
| Mustard | Condiments & Dressings |
| Noodles | Soup, Noodles & Curries |
| Nuts | Popcorn, Nuts, Pretzels & Mixes |
| Package Delivery | Office & School Supplies |
| Pain Relievers | Medical |
| Pancake Mix | Breakfast Food |
| Pencils & Pens | Office & School Supplies |
| Pickles | Oil, Vinegar, Olives & Pickles |
| Pies | Desserts |
| Pizza | Frozen Dinners |
| Potato Chips | Chips |
| Pretzels | Popcorn, Nuts, Pretzels & Mixes |
| Pudding | Dairy Products |
| Relishes | Oil, Vinegar, Olives & Pickles |
| Rice Milk | Milk & Alternatives |
| Salt | Sugar, Spices & Sweeteners |
| School Supplies | Office & School Supplies |

| | |
|---|---|
| Shampoo | Hair Care |
| Shaving Needs | Body Care |
| Shortening | Oil, Vinegar, Olives & Pickles |
| Soft Drinks | Soda |
| Soy Milk | Milk & Alternatives |
| Sports Drinks | Energy Drinks |
| Stuffing Mix | Bread |
| Sun Block | Body Care |
| Syrup | Sugar, Spices & Sweeteners |
| Tahini | Peanut Butter & Jelly |
| Tampons | Feminine Care |
| Tape | Office & School Supplies |
| Tissues | Paper & Paper Products |
| Tofu | Meat Alternatives |
| Toilet Paper | Paper & Paper Products |
| Tomato Paste | Pasta & Sauce |
| Toothbrushes | Dental Care |
| Toothpaste | Dental Care |
| Tuna | Seafood |
| Veggie Burgers | Meat Alternatives |
| Vinegar | Oil, Vinegar, Olives & Pickles |
| Video Games | Toys & Games |
| Waffles | Breakfast Food |
| Whipped Cream | Dairy Products |
| Yogurt | Dairy Products |

# DATA SOURCES

1. American Humane   [americanhumane.org]
2. B Corporation   [bcorporation.net]
3. Berne Declaration   [evb.ch/en]
4. Better World Shopper   [betterworldshopper.org]
5. Business Ethics   [business-ethics.com]
6. Business for Social Responsibility   [bsr.org]
7. Caring Consumer   [caringconsumer.com]
8. Center For Responsive Politics   [opensecrets.org]
9. CEP (Council on Economic Priorities) [archive.org]
10. CERES Principles   [ceres.org]
11. Clean Clothes Campaign   [cleanclothes.org]
12. Clean Computer Campaign   [svtc.igc.org/cleancc]
13. Clean Up Fashion   [cleanupfashion.wordpress.com]
14. Climate Counts   [climatecounts.org]
15. Cornucopia Institute   [cornucopia.org]
16. Corporate Accountability International
      [stopcorporateabuse.org]
17. Corporate Knights   [corporateknights.com]
18. Corpwatch   [corpwatch.org]
19. Covalence EthicalQuote   [covalence.ch]
20. CSRwire   [csrwire.com]
21. Electronics TakeBack Coalition
      [electronicstakeback.com]
22. Ethical Consumer   [ethicalconsumer.org]
23. Ethisphere   [ethisphere.com]
24. Fair Trade Federation   [fairtradefederation.org]
25. Fast Company   [fastcompany.com]
26. Forest Ethics [forestethics.org]

# DATA SOURCES

27. FTSE4Good Global Index  [ftse4good.com]
28. Global Sullivan Principles
    [thesullivanfoundation.org/gsp]
29. Green America  [greenamerica.org]
30. Green Cross International  [gci.ch]
31. Green-e  [green-e.org]
32. Greenopia  [greenopia.com]
33. Greenpeace  [greenpeace.org]
34. Hoover's  [hoovers.com]
35. Human Rights Campaign  [hrc.org]
36. Know More  [knowmore.org]
37. Maquila Solidarity Network  [maquilasolidarity.org]
38. Multinational Monitor  [multinationalmonitor.org]
39. Natural Resources Defense Council  [nrdc.org]
40. Organic Consumers Assn  [organicconsumers.org]
41. New York Times  [newyorktimes.com]
42. Political Economy Research Institute
       [peri.umass.edu]
43. Responsible Shopper  [responsibleshopper.org]
44. Social Venture Network  [svn.org]
45. Socially Responsible Business Awards
       [sociallyresponsibleawards.org]
46. Transfair USA  [transfairusa.org]
47. Union of Concerned Scientists  [ucsusa.org]
48. U.S. Environmental Protection Agency  [epa.gov]
49. Washington Post  [washingtonpost.com]
50. WorldBlu  [worldblu.com]
51. World Environment Center  [wec.org]
52. World Wildlife Fund  [worldwildlife.org]

# About the Author

Since receiving his doctoral degree in sociology from the University of Colorado, Boulder, Ellis Jones has focused all of his energies on bridging the gap between academics, activists and the average citizen. A scholar of social responsibility, global citizenship and everyday activism, Dr. Jones continues to teach and give presentations across the country on how to turn lofty ideals into practical actions. His other work includes *The Better World Handbook* (winner of *Spirituality & Health*'s Best Book of the Year Award for 2002 under the category of Hope).

Dr. Jones has given inspiring yet practical presentations to a wide variety of audiences including colleges and universities, businesses, churches, sustainability symposiums, service conferences and global citizenship summits. He has been interviewed for radio and television in both the US and Canada, and was featured in the documentary film, *50 Ways To Save The Planet.* In 2005, his work inspired the creation of The Better World Handbook Festival in Vancouver, BC. He has lived, studied, and worked in many parts of Europe, Asia, and Central America.

He has won numerous awards for his work in the classroom and currently teaches in the Social Transformation program at Saybrook Graduate School and the Department of Sociology & Anthropology at Holy Cross College in Worcester, MA.

If you are interested in learning more about how you can support this work or would like to schedule a speaking engagement, please send an email to:

doctorjones@betterworldshopper.org

If you have enjoyed *The Better World Shopping Guide*
you might also enjoy other

# BOOKS TO BUILD A NEW SOCIETY

Our books provide positive solutions for people who
want to make a difference. We specialize in:

**Environment and Justice** • **Conscientious Commerce**
**Sustainable Living** • **Ecological Design and Planning**
**Natural Building & Appropriate Technology** • **Nonviolence**
**Educational and Parenting Resources** • **Progressive Leadership**

---

## New Society Publishers
### ENVIRONMENTAL BENEFITS STATEMENT

New Society Publishers has chosen to produce this book on
Enviro 100, recycled paper made with **100% post consumer
waste**, processed chlorine free, and old growth free.

For every 5,000 books printed, New Society saves the following
resources:[1]

| | |
|---:|---|
| 9 | Trees |
| 788 | Pounds of Solid Waste |
| 867 | Gallons of Water |
| 1,130 | Kilowatt Hours of Electricity |
| 1,432 | Pounds of Greenhouse Gases |
| 6 | Pounds of HAPs, VOCs, and AOX Combined |
| 2 | Cubic Yards of Landfill Space |

[1]Environmental benefits are calculated based on research done by the
Environmental Defense Fund and other members of the Paper Task Force
who study the environmental impacts of the paper industry.

---

*For a full list of NSP's titles, please call* **1-800-567-6772**
*or check out our website at:* **www.newsociety.com**

new society
PUBLISHERS

# New Society Publishers

P.O. Box 189

Gabriola Island,

B.C. V0R 1X0

Canada

BOOKS TO BUILD A NEW SOCIETY

Our books provide positive solutions for people who want to make a difference.

For a copy of our catalog, please mail this card to us. We specialize in:

+ Activism
+ Globalization
+ Ecological Design & Planning
+ Environment & Economy

+ Conscientious Commerce
+ Sustainable Living
+ Environmental Education
+ Education & Parenting

+ Progressive Leadership
+ Conflict Education
+ Natural Building &
  Renewable Energy

☐ *Please subscribe me to* NEW SOCIETY NEWS — *our monthly e-mail newsletter.*

Name

Address/City/Province

Postal Code/Zip _____ Email Address

**toll-free 800-567-6772**     **www.newsociety.com**

NEW SOCIETY PUBLISHERS